CW01664214

GREAT CARS

VETERAN AND VINTAGE

Michael Sedgwick

Galley Press

Author	**Michael Sedgwick**
Illustrator	**Mike Atkinson**
Editor/ Designer	**Eric Inglefield**
Consultant	**Michael Ware**

For Christine

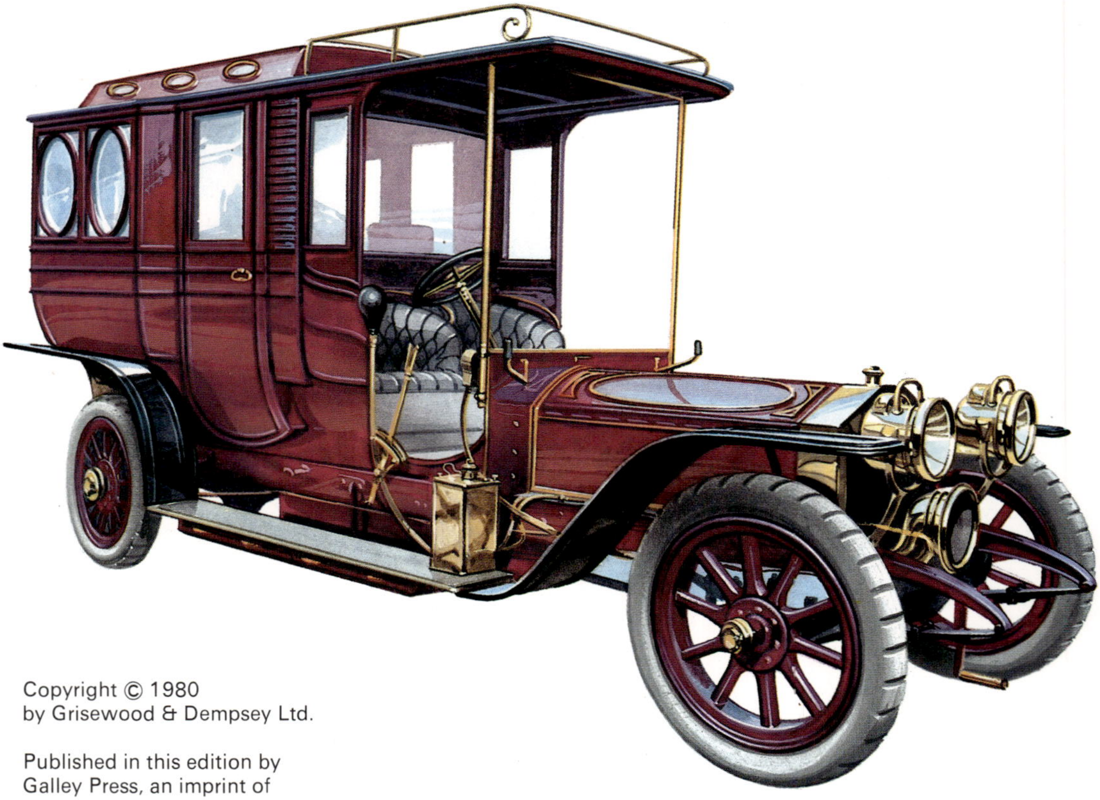

Copyright © 1980
by Grisewood & Dempsey Ltd.

Published in this edition by
Galley Press, an imprint of
W.H. Smith and Son Limited,
Registered No. 237811 England.
Trading as WHS Distributors,
St John's House, East Street,
Leicester, LE1 6NE.

ISBN 0 86136 830 4

All rights reserved. No part
of this publication may be
reproduced, stored in a
retrieval system, or transmitted
in any form or by any means,
electronic, mechanical, photocopying,
recording or otherwise, without
prior written permission from
the publishers.

Printed and bound in Portugal by Printer Portuguesa, Sintra.

Contents

VETERAN CARS

Introduction

In days when we are seeking a replacement for the internal-combustion-engined motor-car, it is sobering to reflect how rapidly it infiltrated our world. A hundred years ago it did not exist. Eighty-five years ago, Peugeot (then one of the world's top three) were happy to have turned out 72 vehicles in a twelvemonth. Yet within another decade, the Peugeot's native France had a potential of around 15,000 units a year, and the United States would break the 25,000 mark in 1906. When the world went to war in 1914, that country already registered over a million automobiles, and was adding half a million annually to the score. Britain had 132,000, with a yearly production potential close to 40,000. French industry was good for 50,000, and even Italy contributed some 10,000 a year. True, neither Japan nor Russia as yet manufactured seriously. In 1912, Greater London registered more cars than the entire Romanov Empire, but the importers of St Petersburg were bringing them in at the rate of 4,000 a year.

Admittedly, outside America the motor-car was still largely the preserve of the rich, and many countries were ill supplied with roads. The Ford succeeded in Asia, South America and Australasia partly because it was cheap, partly because it was foolproof, partly because deliveries were undisturbed by the Great War – but chiefly because its suspension and high ground clearance were admirably suited to bush tracks. Without roads, the automobile could not make headway.

Consider France's leadership in the pioneering years. Latins were maybe less inventive than the Anglo-Saxon races. But they were also less hidebound in their attitudes (a 'horse lobby' never existed in France or Italy); they were also (in France, at any rate) beneficiaries of the admirable Napoleonic *routes nationales*. Germany was the nursery of the internal-combustion engine, and it would be fair to regard the Benz Velo as the first reliable automobile, but true German leadership would not be asserted until the advent of the Mercedes in 1901.

There were also Britain and America – the former the cradle of the Industrial Revolution and the world's iron-master, the latter the home of mass-production built up around the small arms and cheap watch industries. Yet neither led. The United Kingdom, indeed, inflicted a blanket speed limit of 20 mph (32 km/h) as late as 1930. Before that there had been the Locomotives on Highways Act of 1865, with its ossifying limits, not repealed until 1896. A railway-oriented economy, backed by turnpike trusts, were additional deterrents, which explain why early British road vehicles were commercial types – the coaches of Hancock and Gurney and the famed traction engines of Garrett and others. Thomas Rickett's steamers (page 14) were certainly private cars, but they were also technical dead-ends. A Bollée family could never have flourished in England.

Outside the big cities, the United States

◄ *How we expect a Veteran to look. This 16hp, four-cylinder car is one of the bigger 1903 Panhards, with the layout made famous by this firm: engine in front, gearbox amidships, and drive to the rear wheels. Design is untidy: seven exposed banks of tubes form the radiator, driving chains are unprotected from road dirt, and there are no front doors, hood, or windscreen (the two latter were extras). Rear-seat passengers had a door, but it was in the tail panel, as on contemporary horsedrawn vehicles.*

was roadless. It was left to the cycling clubs to proselytize the highways, a state of affairs which explains early cheap car design, and the immense publicity accorded to the early transcontinental marathons. Undoubtedly the industry could have turned out 10,000 mock-Panhards – or even mock-Mercedes – in 1903; there was simply nowhere for them to go.

In 1900 cars were still scarce: but most of the basic technical ideas existed. The automobile engine worked, and it delivered a creditable amount of power, if not very efficiently. Nor is it strictly true to assert that brute force was the governing factor. While racing units progressed from the 3 litres of the later 1890s to 17–20 by 1904–05, the little de Dion single of 1900 was running at 2,000 rpm and giving 6 hp from 500 cc, or 12 bhp per litre. Electric ignition and float-feed carburetters were established, and the mechanically operated inlet valve was soon to appear. Pneumatic tyres were general practice on lighter cars, and some designers, notably the Lanchester brothers, had broken loose from the old concept of the horseless carriage. For all the influence of the *système Panhard* – engine in front, gearbox amidships, and drive to the rear wheels – people were still making cars with rear engines or front-wheel drive. Such geniuses were no anticipators of Porsche or Issigonis: design was strictly functional. Engines went at the back because this was the simplest way to motorize a dog-cart or buggy. Front-wheel drive was another rudimentary form of hippomobile-to-motor conversion, as found on the Lohner electric or the strange Pullcar as late as 1907.

Further, right up to 1905, if not later, the question of motive power was unsettled. Steam and electricity bulked large. They were, after all, known (and harnessed) monsters long before Gottlieb Daimler and Karl Benz translated the ideas of Beau de Rochas and Lenoir into the motor-car engine as we know it today.

There were other attractions, such as greater dependability. There is nothing to go wrong on an electric, while the slow cold-starting rituals of steamers – even in 1909 it could take 35 minutes on a Stanley – were at least sure, and preferable to the ignition and mixture headaches associated with internal combustion.

Then there was the matter of silence. An electric makes no noise; nor, its burner whistle apart, does a steamer, while by direct-coupling the latter's engine to the axle, and mounting the generator at the rear, one could also eliminate smell. The internal-combustion engine vibrated furiously: the price of the little de Dion's efficiency is a tumult which telephones its way up the steering-column. Above all, there were no gears to shift.

In this era of synchromesh and two-pedal automatic, it is hard to comprehend the hurdle of double-declutching, especially on constant-speed engines with no 'gun' to administer during a shift. Much ingenuity – often misplaced – would be directed towards the elimination of this headache. There were simple planetary transmissions which circumvented the dreaded 'side-grubbing of the teeth', there was belt drive such as that retained by Delahaye well into the 20th century, and there were primitive multi-cylindered creatures such as the 1902 CGV, supposed to dispense with a gearbox altogether. No wonder that steam and electricity hung on as long as they did, especially after Serpollet mastered the paraffin burner and did away with the bulk and weight of solid fuels.

Electricity's demise was inevitable, on grounds of range. Batteries were almost as bulky as coal, so the system was soon confined to town runabouts. The advent of electric starting on 1912's Cadillacs was the final nail in the coffin.

Steam sat it out longer, though (Serpollet apart) most of the significant makes were American. Here too, range was a problem, for in pre-condensing days water consumption was formidable. Light runabouts such as the Locomobile carried only enough for 20 miles (32 km), though later condensing systems improved substantially on this. Further, the steamer's excellent acceleration and hill-climbing powers were offset by the limitations of the boiler. A Stanley's 50 mph (80 km/h) could not be sustained for any length of time without a halt to build up pressure. Nor did one ever like sitting on a boiler working at 200 psi or more. Finally, steamers needed more skill to get the best out of them. And as with the electric, self-starters were the last straw.

As for mainstream development of the internal-combustion engine, it is fair to say that the first 15 years of our period (1885–1900) were devoted to making the machine work, the next ten to making it work reliably, and the 1910–14 period to the attainment of perfection. Though there was, of course, a great gulf fixed between the Rolls-Royce, which started 'on the switch' and wafted one up to a remarkably silent 60 mph (100 km/h) and the model-T Ford with its idiosyncratic cold-starting habits, jerky progress, and reluctance to surmount really steep hills in

The structure of very early cars was like that of the horse carriage; the 1897 Cannstatt-Daimler's engine lived in a box like a 'meat-safe' attached to the rear.

A lightweight tubular chassis and wire wheels characterize the 1903 Humberette; front engines were general practice by then.

either of its two forward gears. For less than £200 in Europe, or, say, $900 in America, one did not expect refinement, even if by 1916 trans-Atlantic buyers were dispensing with crank handles and acetylene generators.

The motor-car was taking shape. The most important advances of the early period were the *système Panhard*, the pneumatic tyre, electric ignition, and the mechanically-actuated inlet valve, key to adequate engine control over a wider rev-band. Other developments – the high-speed engine, monobloc casting (which meant shorter and stronger crankshafts), and the selective gear shift – were logical developments. So was shaft drive, which eliminated both the slip- and stretch-prone belt and the chain, the latter's tedious maintenance schedule involving boilings in Russian tallow! Ackermann-type steering was already established: the perilous centre-pivoting front axle was found only on the earliest horseless carriages, notably the 1897 Cannstatt-Daimler.

In the age of the Mini it has become fashionable to decry the Panhard arrangement as a space-waster. So it is, especially when allied to a hefty inline six like the 1910 Napier. But the governing reason for its adoption was weight distribution. The Benz was inherently tail-heavy, and while this was irrelevant at the speeds of which the vehicle was capable, higher velocities, allied to short wheelbases, poor roads, high centres of gravity, and solid tyres, rendered the Panhard configuration imperative if the motor-car were to succeed. It would also wean the vehicle away from its horse-carriage origins, though to the end of our period (in Europe, at any rate) chassis and body were still regarded as separate entities.

Pneumatic tyres were both vital to motoring, and its persistent early bugbear. On the one hand, they smoothed out the ride, permitting higher speeds. On the other, they were the automobile's prime limitation as dependable transport over long distances. The divorce from hippomobile practices meant front and rear wheels of equal diameter, and thus the end of duplicate spares, but throughout our period a tyre life of 2,000 miles (3,200 km) was considered good. The quick-detachable wheel, a 1907 innovation, was not generally used in Europe until 1912–13, and gained little headway in America, where the rising incidence of female motorists would ensure the retention of the more manageable fixed wood type with demountable rim as late as 1931.

Electric ignition heralded the variable-speed engine. The original hot-tube species had been simpler than magnetos (always a closed book to the layman) and independent of batteries, the Achilles' Heel of early coil systems. It did, however, involve a tedious starting ritual. Also high winds (and bad

By 1913 cars were more manageable. A lady driver might, however, find the 12hp Rover hard to crank from cold.

bumps on the road) could blow it out.

So in 1905 one still motored hopefully. The motor-car was tricky to start, and not over-controllable, with its limited rev-band: the usual maximum was about 1,200 rpm. Gear changing was difficult, while cone clutches had to be propped out with a block of wood overnight. Of amenities there were few: weather protection consisted of a cape cart hood and a windscreen. There were no instruments on the dash, and lighting came from an acetylene generator on the running-board. The light was excellent, but the system very vulnerable to rough roads.

Problems of maintenance bulked large. They did more to restrict the spread of automobilism than the actual cost of a vehicle – or its attendant tyre bill. 'Motor servants' were almost a necessity.

The real trouble was that the motor car ingested as much dirt as it showered over passers-by. The elaborate undershielding effected by Spyker was a palliative, but on the early American steam and gas buggies, and on early European *voiturettes* like the Decauville the 'motion' was wholly exposed. It was also under-lubricated, drip-feed systems being messy, and calling for constant attention. Under-oiling spelt seizures: too liberal a manipulation of those fancy brass oilers on the dash laid a smokescreen. Even in 1910, valve gear was often exposed, while gaskets and oil seals were not very effective. The combination of poor lubrication, and the abrasive effects of dust meant decarbonization at 1,000-mile intervals, a laborious affair with fixed-head engines. Not the least of the advantages claimed for the Knight sleeve-valve motor was that it would cover large mileages between decokes.

Cleaning was a chore. Paint and varnish had to be wiped down after every journey, and renewed at yearly intervals. Brass called for constant polishing and there were chains to clean and boil. Nothing was standardized – so much so that among the recommendations put forward for a 'gentleman's motor house' was a screw-cutting lathe. (Cadillac's 1908 standardization test, when three cars were stripped and their parts scrambled before reassembly, created a furore in Europe.) As for garages, these were scarce, and all too often staffed by graduate blacksmiths and cycle dealers who used the local motorist's Benz or Wolseley as a training-ground. Good public transport, however, sometimes helped: British Hotchkiss owners were offered a 24-hour parts service from the Paris factory in 1910.

By 1914, many of the early problems had been solved. Pressure – or at any rate, semi-pressure – lubrication had banished the sight-feed oiler, wheels were detachable, and moving parts better protected from dust, itself on the wane thanks to wider use of tarmac. High-speed engines were gaining ground, and even the average touring unit would run up to 1,600–1,800 rpm. The majority of cars could be had with electric lighting, and Cadillac's electric starter would have become general practice by 1916, but for the war. As it was, in America only Ford held out against it to the end of our period. There was better flexibility, too.

Here the remedy was more cylinders, and thus less shifting. The prentice sixes of Napier and others were bedevilled by the absence of crankshaft balancers, a Lanchester contribution of 1909. One made a six by adding a couple of extra cylinders to a four, and the price of an easy walking pace in top was a tooth-shaking vibration further up the speed range. Crankshaft breakages were common, too – so the six went into temporary eclipse until a new generation of inexpensive Americans, (Buick, Hudson, Studebaker) made their appearance in 1913–14. The vee-eight, with its combination of compactness and flexibility, had been launched on the 1910 de Dion, and Packard followed up in 1915 with a successful V12.

What vital problems remained unsolved? In Europe, a cheap car had yet to emerge. Not so in America, where Ford's single model policy and moving assembly line had rendered outputs of half a million identical cars a year viable. The Europeans had two solutions, neither of them wholly successful.

Today a £175 ($875) Morris sounds a bargain, and it still seems reasonable value by the standards of 1939. But £175 was a lot of money in 1913, and what one got for it was a small four-cylinder engine, maybe electric lighting, and a cruising speed of 30–35 mph (50–60 km/h). The wheels would be detachable, but one still had to crank – and there were only two seats. To make it a four-seater would be asking too much of 15–18 bhp. We were a long way away from the Family Ten of the 1930s.

The other solution was the cyclecar, a barbarous contraption for graduate motorcyclists. Just about the only uncivilized device omitted on it from the early nineties was tube ignition. To a noisy motor-cycle engine would be added cable-and-bobbin steering, belt drive (not always with a free-engine clutch) and plywood construction. One's reward was a £100 automobile capable of an unreliable and comfortless 50 mph (80 km/h).

Brakes, likewise, lagged behind. A 1914 Prince Henry Vauxhall with its lights, starter, wider rev band and excellent handling would in other respects be acceptable today. It can hold 70 mph (112 km/h), the multi-plate clutch is sweet in action, and what enthusiastic driver cares a fig for synchromesh? But its brakes – alas and alack! For a car weighing about 1½ tons in road trim, there are a footbrake working on a drum behind the gearbox, and a handbrake working in drums on the rear wheels. The former, if liberally used, is a fire hazard, and can do dire things to the driveline. The latter will give you some interesting turns in the wet. Four-wheel brakes had already been tried by more than one maker, but since only Argyll used a proper coupled system, the improvement was minimal. Oreste Fraschini of Isotta Fraschini, indeed, admitted that his objective had been faster cornering on the circuit!

Also unborn was the cheap closed car. As long as composite body construction obtained – and Edward G. Budd's all-steel sedan did not see the light of day until 1916 – a closed body cost more, weighed more, and killed performance. It is well to remember, too, that the 35 bhp of today's emission-stifled baby sedans was the norm for a 3-litre in 1914. Thus closed coachwork was reserved for formal carriages and 'doctor's coupés'.

Variety, however, was infinite. An Englishman in 1914 could take his pick, from £90 – 100 cyclecars up to big brutes like the 100 mph Isotta Fraschini. If he fancied steam, Stanleys were available, and Arrol-Johnston had acquired a manufacturing licence for the American Detroit Electric, now with a mock-Renault bonnet full of batteries. The Le Zèbre had only one cylinder: but for £900-odd ($4,500) you could have an eight-cylinder de Dion, all 7.8 litres of it. And even on the real monsters, annual tax was £25 ($125) a year, insurance was not compulsory, and there was no driving test. One just had to remember that – in modern parlance – the footbrake was the hand-brake, and 'revs' did not extend much beyond what we would now term a fast idle.

On its way to Windsor: the first Rickett, 1858

Rickett
1860, Great Britain

Early British road steamers tended to be coaches for public transport rather than private cars. An interesting exception, however, was the machine illustrated above. It was constructed at the Castle Foundry, Buckingham, by Thomas Rickett, one of three or four such vehicles for which he was responsible. His first, made in 1858 for the Marquis of Stafford, is recorded as only a moderate success, though the Prince of Wales showed interest. The car was also demonstrated at Windsor in the presence of Queen Victoria, having arrived from Buckingham under its own power.

Rickett's cars were three-wheelers, with drive to the rear wheels, initially by pitch chain, though a direct-coupled transmission was found on this example, commissioned by the Earl of Caithness in 1860. The driver and two passengers sat on a bench at the front, from which the vehicle was steered, braked, and reversed, the stoker occupying a platform at the rear. Mechanically, the Rickett was a road locomotive, even down to the horizontal boiler. Economy was hardly a strong point: a 90-gallon (450-litre) water supply sufficed for a mere ten miles (16 km), and coal consumption was estimated at 6–10 pounds (2.7–4.5 kg) per mile. Further, the weight in road trim was no less than $2\frac{1}{2}$ tons. In spite of this, the machine comfortably exceeded its design speed of 10 mph (16 km/h), touching 18 mph (29 km/h) on occasion. The steel-spoke wheels seen in the illustration were later replaced by wooden ones, less destructive to road surfaces.

Lord Caithness was clearly of an engineering bent, and in any case the vehicle was destined for his estates in the North of Scotland, too thinly populated to attract any vocal opposition. In August, 1860, he successfully drove his car from Inverness to Thurso, a distance of 150 miles (240 km), accompanied by his wife and the Rev. William Ross. Rickett himself served as stoker. The Earl continued to motor happily in his remote fastnesses until the passing of the Locomotives on Highways Act in 1865 restricted such activities.

Benz

1885, Germany

If we owe the modern internal-combustion engine to Gottlieb Daimler and Karl Benz, the latter must rate as the automobile's true father. Daimler's interests were wider-ranging, and embraced railway and marine engines and stationary machinery.

The son of a locomotive driver from Karlsruhe, who died of pneumonia contracted while on duty, Benz had a hard struggle, training first as a locksmith and then as a locomotive engineer before setting up on his own in 1871. Though he had a two-stroke engine running by 1880, his finances were always insecure, and it was not until two years later that backing from Max Rose and F. W. Esslinger enabled him to pursue his experiments without constant anxiety.

The 1885 three-wheeler reflects some advanced thinking. Though he would later adopt the automatic inlet valve, Benz favoured mechanical actuation for the prototype: he also discarded wind-prone tube ignition in favour of a trembler coil from the start. The horizontal single-cylinder engine was mounted in a tubular frame, with the head pointing forward, and the crankshaft exposed at the rear. The flywheel was also set horizontally. Primary transmission was by belt; a side lever slid this onto a fast pulley when pushed forward, and onto the loose one when pulled back. Brakes were limited to a simple block-type working on the countershaft, and the invalid-carriage-type front fork was unsprung.

Despite a very low output – the first trials gave $\frac{3}{4}$bhp at 400rpm – the Benz ventured onto the public roads in 1886, attaining 8 mph (12 km/h). It was, however, useless on hills, and by 1888, when deliveries began, such refinements as a two-speed gear and front springing had been added. Four-wheelers were in production by 1893, and by the end of the 19th century the breed offered reliable if slow transportation. A total of 572 new Benz cars found buyers in 1899, and the 600 mark was passed a year later.

The exposed 'works' of the Benz with the massive horizontal flywheel which was turned to crank the engine. Also to be seen is the primitive front fork.

Amédée Bollée

1885, France

Although the work of Benz and Daimler was as yet unknown outside Germany, across the border in France the Bollée family, bell-founders of Le Mans, had been developing a series of steam road vehicles since 1873. These varied enormously, from small 'brakes' for personal transport up to the formidable *Marie-Anne* of 1879, a six-wheeled road locomotive rated at 100 hp and capable of hauling 80 tons on the level.

Amédée Bollée senior's first effort, *L'Obéissante* (1873), was good for 25 mph (40 km/h), and featured not only a two-speed sliding-type gear, but two-man operation, the driver being assisted only by a stoker at the rear. In 1876 he built a vehicle with all-independent suspension, a front vertical engine, and a differential back axle. Shaft drive came in 1880, by which time Bollée had appointed a German agent and had orders for 23 vehicles on his books. Unfortunately, the press spread rumours that he was selling to the German Army (bitterness still ran high only a decade after French defeat in the Franco-Prussian War) and French interest faded away. Amédée, however, persisted with some lightweight steam brakes said to do 42 mph (60 km/h).

His son and namesake, at the age of 18, had taken a hand in the game, designing the neat little runabout illustrated below for his personal use – surely the world's first sports car. Its double-acting two-cylinder, slide-valve engine was front-mounted, with a longitudinal crankshaft, and shaft drive to the rear wheels. The car weighed only 1,410 lb (640 kg) and attained 25 mph (40 km/h). He built a second example for his grandfather, which made the Bollées the world's first four-car family, since both Amédée senior and his second son Léon had their own. The two young Bollée brothers would turn to the internal-combustion engine during the ensuing decade.

As a contrast with his son Amédée's 'sports car', the elder Amédée Bollée's 'L'Obéïssante' of 1873 is more in the commercial vehicle idiom favoured by earlier British experimenters; it is what would now be termed a brake for eight or nine passengers, rather than a car for the owner-driver. The vehicle is now displayed in the Conservatoire des Arts et Métiers in Paris.

Duryea progress: the brothers' entry for the London-Brighton Emancipation Run, 1896. Unlike the 1893 prototype, this is not a converted horse-buggy, though the engineering is little changed.

Duryea

1893, United States

In later life the Duryea brothers, Frank and Charles, quarrelled bitterly over their respective contributions to the automobile. In any case, their 1893 prototype now preserved in Washington's Smithsonian Institution was not America's first gasoline-powered vehicle: that honour belongs to the 1891 Lambert. The Duryeas, however, founded the industry by setting up a company to manufacture automobiles in September, 1895.

The basic idea stemmed from Charles, who in 1890 was marketing bicycles made for him by a Massachusetts firm. With $1,000 (£200) financial backing from a certain Erwin Markham, he purchased a secondhand horse-drawn phaeton, which he proposed to motorize on Benz lines, with a horizontal engine and flywheel: Duryea feared that a vertical layout would adversely affect the steering. Burner ignition and a variable friction drive were planned.

Unfortunately, neither engine nor car would work, so during 1892 Frank Duryea was hired. Under his guidance this true horseless carriage was made to function. Charles's two-stroke concept was replaced by a four-stroke single, with automatic inlet valve and low-tension battery ignition. Transmission was by a system of three separate friction clutches giving two forward speeds and a reverse. Shifts were controlled by up and down movement of the steering tiller, but the rear axle was unsprung, the carriage's original transverse full-elliptic spring being retained at the front.

The brothers' second car, built in 1895, was used for experiments with pneumatic tyres, ahead of the European pioneers. On solids, it also won America's first automobile race, from Chicago to Evanston, Illinois. In 1896 the Duryea company succeeded in turning out 13 identical cars for sale, now with belt drive on Benz lines. The basic Duryea theme was continued for several years in three- and four-wheeler forms, latterly with horizontal three-cylinder engines. One of these early Duryeas (complete with armoured fuel tank) became the first motor machine-gun carrier in 1901, while between 1902 and 1906 the make was built under licence for the British market in Coventry.

Neither Duryea brother was associated with any of the big American makers. Frank left to join the Stevens Arms and Tool Company in 1901, producing the limited-production Stevens-Duryea car. Charles's ventures included the odd Buggyaut high-wheeler of 1908, with two-stroke engine, friction drive, and true central control, enabling it to be driven from either seat. As late as 1916 he was still trying to promote obsolete high-wheeler designs in delivery van form.

Panhard
1894, France

To Émile Levassor we owe the layout of the internal-combustion automobile as it was understood for over half a century – an engine at the front, transmitting its power via an amidships-mounted gearbox to the rear axle. (The Bollées, of course, had already applied such principles to steam cars.) The *système Panhard* would be the model for the motor-car for the remainder of the 19th century, while the 'miraculous Mercédès' which supplanted it from 1901 onward was merely a more sophisticated development of the original theme.

The origin of the Panhard concern was a woodworking firm, Périn et Pauwels, established in 1845. Forty years later, the founding partners were dead, and René Panhard, who had replaced Pauwels, brought his friend Levassor into the company. Among Levassor's friends was Édouard Sarazin, who had lately acquired the French rights to the Daimler patents. When he died in November, 1887, these passed to his widow, whom in due course Émile Levassor married.

Levassor began his automobile experiments in 1889; he displayed no interest in belt drive, but tried amidships and rear locations for the engine before finalizing the layout in 1891. At this stage (and up to 1895) exposed gears still featured, cooling was on a total-loss basis, and unlike Benz, Levassor preferred burner ignition. Though solid rubber tyres had replaced iron in 1892, steering was by tiller, the wheel appearing on racers in 1895, and on production models two years later. Final drive was by side chains, while wheelbases were short and the centre of gravity high – a combination that would encompass Émile Levassor's own end.

With the birth of racing in 1894, the tempo quickened. Paris-Rouen was more a reliability trial than anything else, but the best Panhard performance on this occasion, an average speed of 11.1 mph (17.8 km/h) compares interestingly with the 15 mph (24 km/h) achieved by Levassor over the 732-mile (1,170 km) course of Paris-Bordeaux-Paris in 1895. By 1896 the original vee-twin engines of Daimler type had given way to vertical two- and four-cylinder units, the latter rated at 8 hp. By the turn of the century, Panhards of a nominal 12 hp were capable of nearly 50 mph (80 km/h).

Levassor, however, would not live to see the full triumph of his creation. In September, 1896, he set off on his last race, the 1,068-mile (1,700 km) Paris-Marseilles-Paris. His car collided with a dog and overturned, causing injuries to which he succumbed the following year. The company outlived him by 71 years, though there is a certain irony in the reflection that these pioneers of the 'conventional' automobile were among the first to dedicate themselves whole-heartedly to front-wheel drive, which they did in 1946. It is even sadder to record that the vicissitudes of their intriguing little Dyna first drove them into the arms of Citroën, and then, in 1967, into oblivion.

A youthful C. S. Rolls with his 1898 racing Panhard. Noteworthy are wheel steering and pneumatic tyres.

The controls of a 1903 7 hp Panhard, showing the make's characteristic 'barrel' controls on the steering wheel.

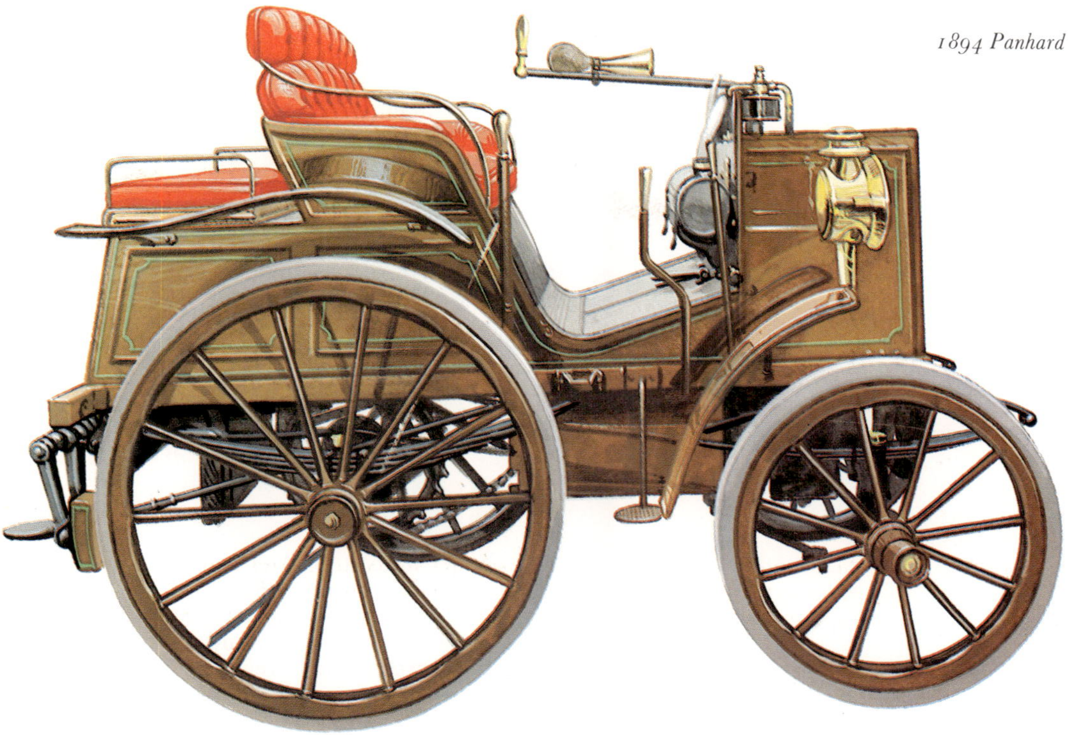

1894 Panhard

A World War I photograph of the Abbé Gavois with his Panhard, by then nearly a quarter of a century old, and which he himself had bought secondhand in 1894!

Léon Bollée Tricar
1896, France

C. S. Rolls at the controls of his Bollée Tricar. The passenger impeded forward vision and was first to bear the brunt of any accident.

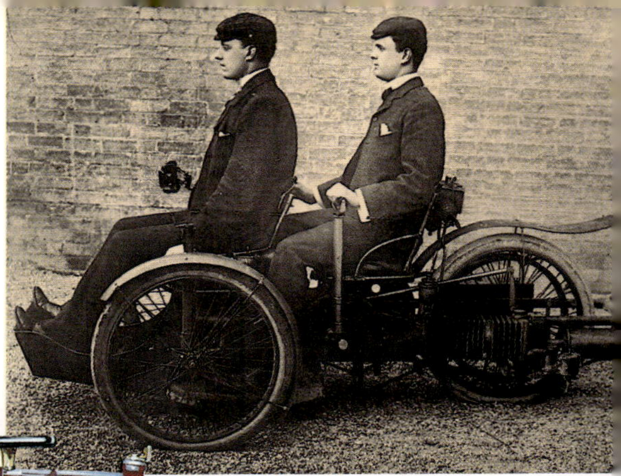

1896 Léon Bollée Tricar

Some of the hazards of the early motor-car were highlighted by Émile Levassor's accident in 1896 (see page 18). Something lower and lighter was clearly desirable. The 1896 Léon Bollée tricar had at least both these merits: weight was a mere 448lb (200kg). In the 1897 Paris-Dieppe race Jamin's example averaged 25.2mph (40.3km/h), as against the 24.6mph (39.4km/h) of the big de Dion steamer, and the 23.1mph (36.9km/h) of the fastest Panhard.

Refinement was, however, totally absent. Here was a tandem-seater with single driven rear wheel, based on a steel-tube frame. The passenger sat in front, vulnerable to any accident. Of springs there were none: the single-cylinder horizontal engine with its burner ignition was rear-mounted. The driver's right hand controlled a small steering-wheel: his left coped with a spade handle. This, when pushed forward, slid the driving wheel back to tighten the belt: rearward movement loosened it, while rotation of the handle selected the three forward speeds. The footbrake worked directly on the flywheel, and only the barrel of the cylinder was finned, hence overheating was common. No clutch was provided: one 'paddled off', in motor-cycle style.

A rousing and noisy 30mph (50km/h), however, presented no other problems, and the Bollée carried all before it until racing rules were amended to raise the minimum weight limit for *voiturettes*, and to stipulate side-by-side seating for the crew.

Cannstatt-Daimler 4hp
1897, Germany

Though Gottlieb Daimler had motorized a boneshaker bicycle and had a primitive four-wheeler on the road in 1886, he was slower off the mark than Benz with series production. It was not until 1895 that Daimlers began to appear in any quantity; this early type was made until 1901.

Despite its wheel steering, the Daimler was primitive in every other way, resembling a horsedrawn carriage minus shafts and horse. Unlike Benz's cars, it used tube ignition, while the steering was of non-Ackermann type with centre-pivoting front axle, even if this were no hazard at such low operating speeds. Brakes were likewise somewhat equestrian: a pedal-operated wooden block on the counter-shaft supplemented by a spoon device on the rear wheels. The engine, an inline twin, lived in a box like a meat-safe at the rear. Four pulleys attached to the crankshaft transmitted motion by four flat leather belts to the countershaft, and thence to pinions meshing with toothed rings on the rear wheels. Cooling water was fed to the inside of the hollow fly-wheel. The coil springs at the rear were interposed between chassis and body: the engine, in an angle-iron frame attached to the latter, suffered from up-and-down movement on rough roads, accentuating the tendency of the burners to blow out.

1897 De Dietrich 9hp

De Dietrich 9hp

1897, France

Even though the combination of front engine and rear-wheel drive was gaining acceptance by 1897, not everyone was content with the *système Panhard* (see page 18). The de Dietrich, designed by Amédée Bollée junior of steam-voiturette fame for the famous Franco-German railway equipment makers, was afflicted with alarming complexities.

The twin-cylinder automatic inlet valve engine was mounted horizontally with the heads pointing forward, but the transmission of its modest output pursued a devious rearward course. A belt on the nearside of the countershaft had the usual fast and loose pulleys, on which four gears meshed with four further gears on a parallel shaft incorporating a differential. By this time the driveline was aft of the wheels, so any remaining power which had survived the transmission journey now had to come forward again via bevel gears and short universal-jointed shafts to a second pair of bevels! Even then the drive had to be turned through 90 degrees to a final set of bevels incorporated in the wheels.

The de Dietrich also had tube ignition, total-loss cooling from a water tank under the front seat, and a sight-feed lubrication system which coped with only one of the engine's main bearings. The pedal-operated reverse had to be held in by continuous pressure. Later improvements included proper tubular radiators (1898), chain final drive in 1901, and electric ignition by 1902. A total of 500 had been sold by the end of 1901. The car also did well in commercial form: a $3\frac{1}{2}$-ton truck built in 1899 attained 9mph (14km/h) and could climb a 1-in-9 gradient with full load.

◄ *The rear doors give access to the Cannstatt-Daimler's twin-cylinder engine.*

1897 Cannstatt-Daimler 4hp

De Dion-Bouton $4\frac{1}{2}$hp

1900, France

By the turn of the present century the modern light car was emerging. By the end of 1902 de Dion-Bouton had made 33,000 of their single-cylinder high-speed engine, were selling 2,000 *voiturettes* a year, supplying motors to countless motor-cycle and car firms, and had a formidable backlog of orders.

When Benz and Daimler had been content with 500–600 rpm, de Dion units ran at over three times this speed. They were also vastly more efficient – nearly 2 bhp from 250 cc in 1896, while the first car units extracted 3.5 bhp from 402 cc. True, a rear engine might seem a retrograde step in the *système Panhard*'s heyday; so did the *vis-à-vis* seating of pre-1902 de Dions, on which front passengers faced the driver and obstructed his view. But the vehicle was simple; it was also foolproof.

The basis of the car was a tubular frame, at the rear of which the single-cylinder engine was set vertically: on early models only the head was water-cooled. Drive was transmitted to the rear wheels via a two-speed constant-mesh gear with separate expanding clutches. The weight was carried on a tubular dead axle, curved to pass below the final drive

Before the days of the honeycomb radiator, badges were rarely seen on cars. de Dion-Bouton mounted their emblem on the side, and the brass script at the front.

The bonnet on this modernized de Dion is a dummy: the game is given away by the side-mounted starting handle.

housing bolted to the frame. Ignition was by a coil of non-trembler type.

Driving was simplicity itself. The absence of a conventional clutch eliminated that all-too-familiar 'side-grubbing of the teeth', and lubrication was taken care of by a hand pump, given a quick squirt to four positions at 15–20 mile (20–30 km) intervals. In place of a hand or foot throttle, de Dion used a decelerator which actuated a transmission brake when depressed to its limit. On such a compact machine a reverse was scarcely necessary, but a pedal-operated device was added early in the car's production life.

Even the first $3\frac{1}{2}$ hp cars could exceed 20 mph (32 km/h), and the enlarged $4\frac{1}{2}$ hp of 1900 was appreciably faster. In 1900 the makers claimed that their clientele included five princes, two dukes, nine marquises, and nineteen counts and countesses. Light vans were available: one firm of brewers even operated a 'product-mobile', on which the sidelamps were shaped like beer mugs and the driver sat inside a mock bottle, the label taking the form of a sheet of transparent glass–surely the world's first curved screen! The engine was listed in marine form, selling for £100 ($500) complete with mounting frame and reverse gear. A branch was opened in New York, offering complete cars for as little as $800.

Inevitably conventional influences moved in. Dummy bonnets had been seen on the rear-engined cars by 1902, while later that year the power unit was moved to the front, and subsequent singles could be had with orthodox, sliding-type three-speed gearboxes. The basic two-speeders, however, retained their following (notably in the medical profession) and were still being made, automatic inlet valves and all, as late as 1910.

The Locomobile had a direct chain drive without gears, but there was no protection from road dust or mud.

Locomobile Steam Runabout

1900, United States

If the internal-combustion engine was already accepted in Europe for light cars, America was not so firmly committed. Here the role of such vehicles was limited to town work, and the same buggy-like structure with its piano box body on a light reach-bar frame sufficed, whatever the motive power. Some firms even offered a choice of gasoline, steam, or electricity.

Designed by the Stanley brothers, who had then sold their patent rights for $250,000 (£50,000), the Locomobile was a very early example of true volume production, sales building from 750 in 1900 to a peak of 2,750 two years later. W. M. Letts's London agency managed to unload 400 in two seasons. This was not surprising, since for £190 ($950), later cut to £150 ($750), the little runabout offered silence and a 20 mph (32 km/h) cruising gait, with no gears to shift. The 'works' consisted of a vertical fire-tube boiler below the seat, and a two-cylinder simple engine driving direct to the rear axle by chain. The driver's right hand coped with engine and burner controls, steering was by tiller, and a pedal-operated band brake worked on the rear axle. In a disaster situation one reversed the engine, though if the chain broke, all means of slowing down ceased abruptly.

Snags were numerous. The burner was lit by a firing iron which had to be heated over a stove. If the fire went out on a journey, bundles of petrol-soaked rags were a poor substitute. The 15-gallon (75-litre) water tank gave a range of only 20 miles (32 km) between refills, and Hubert Egerton reckoned that on his British end-to-end drive of 1900 he had consumed the equivalent of five tons of the liquid. The entire motion was exposed, and road dust was never the best of lubricants. No wonder Locomobile elected to switch to the internal-combustion engine in 1903, though a year earlier they and their principal steam rivals (Mobile, Toledo, and White) had accounted for more than half the cars registered in New York State.

Lohner-Porsche

1900, Austria

Electrically-powered vehicles provided a choice of gears, and remained popular for much longer with the urban motorist, though the majority of such vehicles were chauffeur-driven broughams. Jacob Lohner, an old-established Viennese coachbuilder and supplier of coaches to the House of Habsburg, took the logical step in 1896, when he launched into self-propelled machinery to the design of a youthful Ferdinand Porsche.

Initially the concept was quite simply that of the *avant-train*, on which the steering axle of an existing horse-drawn carriage was replaced by an electric motor with spur gear drive to the front wheels. The batteries were housed under the coachman's box, four forward speeds were provided, and an operational range of 25–50 miles (40–80 km) was claimed.

In 1900, however, Porsche improved on this by mounting the motors in the front hubs, thus eliminating a complex drive train. For greater traction, four-wheel drive was offered, this doubling output from five to ten horsepower. A special tandem-seated car with streamlined nose was used by the designer himself to take the Semmering Hill Climb record, though this 10-kilometre uphill run at maximum speed represented the limit of battery endurance. Such was the load carried that this sprint car turned the scales at around three tons. On electric cars, power brakes served the same function as a steam car's reverse. There was also a special generator switch to enable the batteries to be partially recharged while coasting downhill.

From 1902, Porsche turned his attention to 'mixed' systems on which a petrol engine drove a dynamo to power his hub motors. This coped with charging problems at the price of further complexity, and though his Mercédès-Mixte cars ran in sprints, the future for both this type and for the Lohner-Porsche electric lay in the realm of commercial vehicles. Among types announced in 1908 were a rear-drive electric ambulance of conventional 'bonneted' appearance for Hanover, and a series of front-wheel drive fire engines for Berlin.

An example of early four-wheel drive, this Lohner-Porsche fire engine was operating in London in about 1910. Similar ones were in use in Vienna.

Mercedes 35hp
1901, Germany

Wilhelm Maybach's Mercedes was the automobile sensation of 1901. If one draws modern parallels, it was the Rolls-Royce and Ferrari of its day, making a spectacular appearance in the 1901 Nice-Salon-Nice race with a winning average of 36.63 mph (58.6 km/h) over a long and hilly course. It rendered the Panhard – if not the Panhard system (see page 18) – obsolete overnight, and within two years such firms as Star in Britain, Berliet in France, Martini in Switzerland, and Fiat in Italy were turning out convincing imitations of the design.

New departures were, of course, pressed-steel frames, honeycomb radiators in place of the Panhard's clumsy, unframed, nest of tubes, mechanically operated inlet valves, low-tension magneto ignition in place of burners, and a selective, gate-type gearchange instead of the progressive quadrant. None of

The 'office' of an early Mercedes. As a hand throttle was fitted, there are only two pedals, but the selective 'gate' gear change is visible, as is the sight-feed lubricator on the dash. Oil sidelamps of horse-carriage type sufficed.

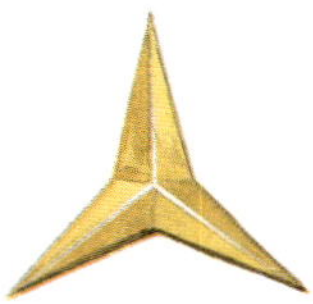

The three-pointed star that is still the emblem of today's Mercedes-Benz.

Mercédès Jellinek, who gave her name to the Mercedes motor-car.

◄*Old and new design: an early 35hp Mercedes (right) with a contemporary twin-cylinder Panhard (left). The contrast in radiators is noteworthy.*

these was entirely new. Daimler of Germany had fitted honeycombs on their 1896 truck and on their little-known PD *voiturette* of 1899. In this latter year, the 24hp Phönix-Daimler racer featured a pressed-steel chassis and gate change, though its short wheelbase and high build gave it a well-substantiated reputation for vicious handling. And even if a Mercedes engine turned at little over half the speed already achieved by de Dion's tiny singles, it offered a high degree of engine control with its combination of valve gear, ignition, and Maybach's efficient float-feed carburetter. The lower centre of gravity made it safer to drive than the old Panhards.

Its dual personality–as racer and luxury tourer–was international, thanks to the energetic efforts of Emil Jellinek, the Austro-Hungarian Consul in Nice. He acted as an unofficial agent, selling Daimlers to his friends. The car rightly bore his daughter's name, for it could scarcely have happened without his sizable backing and a firm order for 36 of the new type.

Output of the 5.9-litre, pump-cooled engine, with its twin side camshafts, was 35bhp at 1,000rpm, and the drive was transmitted via a four-speed gearbox and scroll clutch to the usual exposed side chains. The frame rode on four semi-elliptic springs, and the foot-brake worked on the transmission; it was kept cool by water from an underfloor-mounted tank. Fuel was fed from a rear tank by exhaust pressure, with an auxiliary hand pump for starting. The car retained sight-feed lubrication, by a battery of oilers on the dash, and the wheels were still of unequal diameter front and rear, which meant that spare tyres had always to be duplicated.

A Mercedes was an expensive plaything. By the time the breed reached Britain in 1902, the improved 40hp cost £2,000 ($10,000), and a further £800 ($4,000) would be asked for the monstrous 9.2-litre Sixty of 1903. In return for this, the owner had a potential race winner that would outrun anything else on the road. The real problem was, of course, tyre consumption. Top speed of a 35 in road trim was around 50mph (80km/h), though Sixties could top the 70 mark.

This badge appeared only on Scania-Vabis products from 1911. It commemorates, however, the chain wheel of Scania bicycles and the eagle emblem of Scania's home city, Malmö.

1902 Scania

Scania
1902, Sweden

Sweden was as yet infertile soil for the new form of locomotion. Roads were poor, and the winter climate savage. Thus Swedish engineers tended to be more interested in commercial vehicles, which had a useful potential as feeders to a scattered railway network. Of the country's three major manufacturers in early days–Scania of Malmö, Vabis of Sodertälje, and Tidaholm–the two former (who merged in 1911) were always better known for their trucks, while Tidaholm made virtually nothing else.

Scania had been founded in 1894 to make British Humber bicycles under licence. Their first experimental cars appeared in 1901, from the drawing-board of Fridolf Thorssin. They were powered by single-cylinder aircooled engines of German Kämper make, set transversely underfloor at the rear. Drive was taken via a two-speed epicyclic gearbox to a central chain.

During 1902, water cooling was tried on a vehicle which conformed, predictably, to the *système Panhard*. Its twin-cylinder engine, still a Kämper product, lived under a frontal bonnet, and the driveline now embraced a three-speed gearbox and side chains. Scania also tried another aircooled unit of Swedish make, though in the 1905–10 period design settled down, with emphasis on conventional watercooled fours, made in very small numbers. Nor did the merger with Vabis lead to any increased interest in private cars: between 1906 and 1924 (when the group finally devoted itself to trucks) a mere 485 were turned out. Until the advent of the Volvo in 1927, Swedes were content to rely on the United States and Germany for their personal transport.

Wolseley 10hp
1902, Great Britain

Mass production was a long way away in Britain in 1902, when the country's largest maker, Wolseley, had a potential of some 500 cars a year: in 1901 they had delivered 323. The firm, originally makers of sheep-shearing machinery and now owned by the Vickers ordnance empire, had entered the automobile industry in 1895, with the appointment of Herbert Austin to take charge of the new department. From experimental, Bollée-inspired tricars, he had progressed by 1899 to a four-wheeler with horizontal single-cylinder engine, belt primary drive to a three-speed gearbox, and side-chain final drive. This had performed with distinction in the Thousand Miles' Trial of 1900, and series production followed.

Wolseleys were distinguishable by their side-cranking horizontal engines, the twin-cylinder versions being set across the frame. Ignition was by twin coils, and lubrication by drip feeds. The primary belt had, however, been scrapped in favour of a chain, and the gearbox was given four forward speeds. The pressed-steel frame incorporated four cross-members, and as usual the footbrake worked on the transmission. Production Wolseleys, unlike the 1899 prototype, had wheel steering.

Certainly the cars were not under-cooled, since the radiator area wrapped round the low bonnet, with vertical, interconnected water tanks on either side. The engines were very slow-turning: this 10 hp model delivered its maximum power at 700 rpm, while the progressive gearchange was also very slow, and modern drivers would be confused by the right-hand clutch pedal. Apart from a tendency to break crankshafts when hard pressed, Wolseleys were, however, very reliable, and reasonably priced. A 5 hp single-cylinder two-seater cost £250 ($1,250) and the 10 hp tonneau £380 ($1,900).

Further development presented technical problems. While it is possible to mount two cylinders transversely side-by-side, the demand for a four led to the adoption of a horizontally-opposed arrangement on the bigger 24 hp. In any case, the Mercedes idiom was now in fashion. Wolseley's flat-four racers had a good record, beating the faster Napiers (if not the Continental opposition) in the last two Gordon Bennett Races of 1904 and 1905, but Austin's directors demanded a vertical engine. When he refused to countenance such ideas, they first hired John Davenport Siddeley to design one for them – and then fired Austin. He promptly set up his own company – to manufacture a 25/30 hp four with vertical cylinders!

An early use of a windscreen and fixed top on a 1902 Wolseley.

1902 Wolseley 10 hp

One way of securing an adequate cooling surface was to extend the radiator tubes round the sides of the bonnet, a characteristic of Austin's horizontal-engined Wolseleys.

Lanchester 12 hp

1903, Great Britain

In the days of Mercedes dominance, the Lanchester might seem to have had a 'horseless' appearance. Almost alone among cars of its period, however, it was designed as an entity, and not just as a chassis to be handed to a coachbuilder capable of inflicting the ultimate in bulk and weight upon it.

Frederick Lanchester and his brother George designed from scratch, without reference to any Panhard ideas. Among the 'firsts' that stand to their credit are a direct drive on top gear in 1896 (an innovation usually ascribed to Louis Renault), silent worm drive, cantilever springs and foot accelerators in 1897, detachable wire wheels and preselective gear change in 1901, and full-pressure lubrication as early as 1904. If true unitary structures lay in the future, the lower part of a Lanchester body was integral with the frame members, giving a structural stiffness seldom encountered in this era. This was further reinforced by the transversely mounted fuel tank, while the unconventional Lanchester-built body was in fact highly practical. On pre-1914 models the engine lived between the front seats, thus saving space and giving excellent forward vision. Dashboard and front wings hinged up to improve access, and the entire rear tonneau of the 1903 car, illustrated below, was detachable, turning it into a two-seater.

Early cars used horizontally-opposed two-cylinder aircooled engines, with mechanically-operated overhead valves: a good balance was assured by the use of two superimposed crankshafts. Ignition was by low-tension magneto, and Lanchester's wick carburetter was dirt-proof. To back up the refinements of the worm drive and cantilever springing, the brothers fitted a crash-proof epicyclic gearbox with central lever control, on the principle of a modern preselector. Even the out-of-date tiller steering was quick, and had the merit that one pointed the lever in the desired direction. By 1903 Lanchester were in process of abandoning the air cooling of early days in favour of a water pump. This apparent concession to orthodoxy in fact added another 2 bhp, hitherto absorbed by the twin fans.

The 1903 12 hp car weighed 2,436 lb (1,106 kg), and attained almost 40 mph (65 km/h). It was quieter than most of the opposition and consumed fuel at a reasonable 20 mpg (14 lit/100). Unfortunately, the Lanchesters were constantly beset by commercially-minded directors who demanded that their cars fell into line with rival models. Tiller steering was dropped in 1909 to cope with the growing weight of the latest four- and six-cylinder types. These multi-cylinder units also called for a vertical mounting, albeit still between the front seats. On 1915's Sporting Forty there was even a conventional bonnet, though epicyclic transmission and worm drive survived. Yet as early as 1904, a South African motorist claimed that his Lanchester was the least tiring of all cars, could put 250 miles (400 km) into a day's run, and returned 24 mpg (12 lit/100) even under such conditions.

1903 Lanchester 12 hp

A Lanchester advertisement of 1903 stresses a hill-climb victory but says nothing of the fancy, detachable brougham top, an optional extra.

On the War Office's Lanchesters a different form of weather cover was used: a reversible Victoria top for the officers at the back.

An unusual front end: the sloping 'apron' and lack of a conventional bonnet identify pre-1905 Lanchesters.

37

Oldsmobile Curved Dash Runabout

1903, United States

Henry Ford may have pioneered the moving assembly line, but real mass-production began in 1902 when Ransom Eli Olds turned out 2,500 Curved Dash Runabouts in a year. Thereafter deliveries climbed steadily to their peak of 6,500 units in 1905 before fading away under the influence of more modern designs such as Ford's four-cylinder Model-N.

Olds had realized that a cheap runabout must be simple, and his slogan was 'Nothing to Watch but the Road'. And watching the road was easy, since the Oldsmobile, like the Locomobile steamers it had supplanted, was little more than a buggy with shafts and horse removed, and a power train unobtrusively inserted underneath the structure. Vision was unobstructed. The chassis, too, was pure buggy: a short frame linked to front and rear axles by quarter-elliptic springs, and reinforced at the front by a transverse full-elliptic arrangement. Steering was by tiller. The horizontal single-cylinder engine lived amidships, delivering its output at a sedate 500 rpm, or 'one chuff per telegraph pole', suitably muffled by an enormous silencer. The two forward ratios of the planetary gearbox were selected by hand: they were also widely spaced, low being very low indeed, and needed even on the gentlest of hills.

The Oldsmobile's leisurely performance on country roads might suggest that it was suitable only as an urban runabout. This was disproved in 1903, when Whitman and Hammond not only drove a Curved Dash Runabout from San Francisco to New York, but managed it in 73 days.

The model survived its production run with little change, though the engine was enlarged and uprated to 7 hp in 1904, and some later versions sprouted dummy bonnets and conventional radiators. Ford had, however, successfully mated a modern four-cylinder power unit to the two-speed transmission in 1906, selling the result for $500 (£100), $50 less than a contemporary Oldsmobile. Thereafter the traditional gas buggies faded away.

The Oldsmobile's sedate and uncomplicated motion was well suited to the elderly, though they would have paid extra for a patent leather hood.

Daimler 28/36hp

1904, Great Britain

Daimler of England have long been associated with royalty, funeral corteges, and stately limousines, By contrast, the cars made in the first decade of the 20th century had a marked sporting flavour. Company advertising centred round 'weekly wins' in sprints and hill-climbs: these were recorded in America as well as in Europe.

The 1904 models signalled recovery from shaky finances that had plagued the firm's early years. They also marked the advent of the famous fluted radiator, three-piece alligator bonnet, and such minor distinguishing features as a push-on rather than pull-on handbrake lever and a slatted wooden shield protecting the petrol tank. As all these characteristics survived for many years, it is sometimes difficult to date a Daimler, even though the side-chain drive was dropped after 1908.

In many respects the Daimler followed the established Mercedes theme. Inlet valves were mechanically operated, though British technique was more advanced than German in that Daimler's engineers opted for the single-camshaft L-head type from the start. Coil ignition was standard: magnetos, when fitted, were of the high-tension type. The four-speed selective-shift gearboxes, transmission and rear-wheel brakes, and exhaust pressure fuel feed followed accepted practice. Daimler, however still used tubular radiators, and clung to the old armoured-wood frame until 1906. The 5.7-litre engine's 36 bhp compares closely with the 35 bhp of the slightly bigger 1901 Mercedes, a fact that indicates the German car's *avant-garde* thinking.

'Distinctively different'—even in 1904. This was the first year for Daimler's famous fluted radiator and the legendary three-piece alligator bonnet. The front end would have looked much the same ten years later.

The 1905 competition season proved the Daimler's worth, with six fastest times of the day and seven class wins in Britain alone, not to mention another class victory in the hill-climb section of the German Herkomer Trophy Trials. By 1906, the biggest Daimler ran to a herculean 10.6 litres, and nothing smaller than a 6.8-litre was available. Perhaps unfortunately, the company espoused the Silent Knight sleeve-valve engine in 1908, and though this ensured them a generous share of the chauffeur-driven dowager market, it also meant that half a century would elapse before the world saw another true sports Daimler.

Darracq Flying 15

1904, France

Today we should regard the Flying 15 Darracq as a sports car. A speed of over 45 mph (72 km/h) from a touring 3-litre selling in Britain for less than £500 ($2,500) is remarkable when one compares it with the 10 hp Wolseley of 1902.

Alexandre Darracq was another graduate from the cycle industry, from which he was bought out in 1896 by a British combine. He then set up in business making cycle components, with brief sallies into electric cabs, rotary-engined motor-cycles, and an unfortunate belt-driven Bollée four-wheeler, before coming up with a more practical shaft-driven lightweight in 1900. This had a tubular frame, 785 cc single-cylinder engine, three-speed gearbox, and bevel drive. An unusual feature was the column-mounted gearshift found on most Darracqs up to 1907.

Darracq sold 1,200 units during their first season, subsequently adding a range of twins and fours. These bigger cars had achieved mechanically-operated inlet valves by 1902, while on the Flying 15 there was a further innovation, a one-piece stamped steel frame. Otherwise the car was orthodox, with pair-cast cylinders, and dual ignition with eight plugs. Springs were semi-elliptic at front and rear.

The Flying 15 made its name in long-distance marathons. In America, Darracq importer F. A. La Roche ran his car 2,350 miles (3,760 km) in 14 days without stopping the engine, whereupon, on the far side of the Atlantic, Archibald Ford capped his achievement by covering much the same mileage in just over eight days.

Franklin Model-A

1904, United States

Even if design had yet to settle down in 1904, the American Franklin was 'different', with its vertical-four aircooled engine, full-elliptic springing, and liberal use of aluminium–for bodies and differential casings–in pursuit of designer John Wilkinson's passion for weight saving. Later he would use chassis frames of ash, though a subframe of angle iron is still found on the 10 hp car illustrated opposite. The engine is set across the frame, Mini-fashion, though the resemblance goes no further, since the drive is transmitted via a two-speed, lever-controlled planetary gearbox and a central chain to the rear axle. Initially, Franklins had only a single contracting band brake on the differential, and the pedal-operated reverse was the official emergency system. By 1904, however, there were two sets of brakes on the rear wheels.

Franklin's slogan 'Scientific light weight' was no idle boast. A two-seater Franklin weighed 1,100 lb (500 kg), the same as a Curved Dash Oldsmobile and 200 lb (90 kg) less than a comparable Cadillac, both of them, of course, watercooled. Thus performance was appreciably superior to an Oldsmobile's, as was shown when Whitman and Carris crossed the North American Continent in only 33 days. The Franklin did 40 mph (64 km/h), and 36 mpg (7.9 lit/100). Sales in 1904 were an impressive 701 units. From 1905 Franklin began the switch to longitudinal engines, still aircooled.

◄ *On a modern steering-column change there are no visible notches on the quadrant, as there are on the 1904 Darracq.*

1904 Kriéger

Kriéger
1904, France

Over the years electric cars changed little, retaining their hippomobile style. Kriéger, their noted French exponent, started his career, like Jacob Lohner, with a line of *avant-train* conversions for horse-drawn carriages. Some of these had electric power steering, more than half a century ahead of the big American manufacturers. A Kriéger taxicab was operating in Paris by the end of 1898. Production models retained front-wheel drive by spur gears, the front axle riding on full-elliptic springs. The two electric motors developed a total of 6 hp, while a goodly proportion of the 3,200-lb (1,400-kg) weight was contributed by the batteries: when Kriéger attempted a 'long-distance' model in 1900, the result was a 2½-tonner. Early models had wire-rope brakes on the front wheels, which rendered the electric back-up system all the more vital.

In 1904 output was quoted as 9 bhp, and the driver had six forward speeds and two reverses at his disposal. Speed was 15 mph (24 km/h) and range 56 miles (90 km), though a lightweight (760-kg or 1,680-lb) two-seater Electrolette managed 70 miles between recharges.

Kriéger, like Porsche, fell for the attractions of petrol-electrics, listed alongside the standard cars from 1903 onward. The latter could now be had with dummy bonnets (though still with driven front wheels) in 1906. Kriéger battery-electrics were also made under licence in Germany and Italy. In 1908, however, the company was in liquidation.

1904 Franklin Model-A

Horch 18/22 hp
1905, Germany

This Horch is typical of 1905, though on a high-performance car shaft drive represents advanced thinking. Gear and handbrake levers are mounted together on the right-hand side; there are no front doors; wheels and rims are both non-detachable; and oil and acetylene lamps are used.

German technical progress was aided and abetted by such long-distance rallies as the Herkomer Trophies (1905–6) and Prince Henry Trials (1907–10). An energetic supporter of such events was August Horch, who built the winner of the 1906 Herkomer, and produced a remarkable streamliner for the 1908 Prince Henry, with dual-cowl four-seater body, cowled radiator, and pontoon running-boards: even the spare tyres were neatly faired into the tail. Horch claimed that these improvements were worth 6 bhp in engine performance, but his directors disapproved of money spent on competitions, and fired him a year later.

Horch belonged to a new generation of trained engineers, having been Karl Benz's works manager at Mannheim for three years (1896–9) before setting up on his own. His 2.7-litre four-cylinder 18/22 was typical of its period. Engine speeds were going up, and the car's overhead-inlet-valve unit developed its maximum power at 1,400 rpm. Ignition was by high-tension magneto, and shaft drive had supplanted chains, except on the biggest cars. The leather cone clutch, exhaust pressure fuel feed, pressed steel frame and four-speed gearbox were regular practice. In competition trim speeds higher than the advertised 70 km/h (45 mph) were possible.

1905 Lacoste et Battmann 6 hp

Lacoste et Battmann 6 hp
1905, France

One seldom heard of this make outside its native France. Yet a vast and complex range of singles, twins and fours from 4½ to 40 hp was offered. Engines were to customer's choice: the only sure thing was that they were not made by Messrs Lacoste and Battmann!

While suppliers of proprietary components were firmly established in 1905 – de Dion and Aster made engines for countless small firms – Lacoste et Battmann went even further. They sold a complete car – to which the nominal maker added paint, trim, and a data plate (radiator badges were not yet in fashion). You had the bonnet you fancied: 'Panhard' or 'Mercedes' styles in early days, giving way later to imitations of Delaunay-Belleville and Gobron-Brillié. The single-cylinder Lacoste runabout featured an armoured-wood chassis with tubular subframe for engine and gearbox, outboard rear springs, and a bevel-drive back axle. The sliding-type gearbox came with two or three forward speeds.

The make had eight certain British aliases in 1904, and could be had in 1905 as an Anglian, Cupelle, Gamage, Jackson, Régal or Speedwell. Gamages might observe piously that their *voiturette* 'cannot be purchased elsewhere under another name', but often a reluctance to spend money on their own advertising illustrations gave the game away. The price of a 6 hp two-seater in 1905 could be anything from £130 ($650) to £150 ($750).

White 15 hp
1905, United States

While the light steam buggies faded from the American scene in about 1904, Rollin H. White's more sophisticated models (with water-tube instead of fire-tube boilers, and instantaneous steam generators of semi-flash type) had a longer run; they accounted for over 9,000 vehicles in the first decade of the 20th century. The first Whites had the reach-bar frames, exposed motion and chain drive of the early Stanley-Locomobile family, though automatic lubrication was used as early as 1901. Wheel steering, and conventional armoured wood chassis riding on semi-elliptic springs, came in 1903. The double-acting compound engine was mounted under a gasoline-type bonnet at the front, though the boiler still lived under the front seat.

Whites were now shaft-driven, looked like gasoline cars even down to frontal 'radiators' (condensers) and could match them on performance, doing 15 mpg (18.8 lit/100) on fuel and 8.3 mpg (about 33 lit/100) on water, with a range between refills of 80–100 miles (130–160 km). Controls followed petrol-car style with brake and pressure pump to the driver's right, though he had also to cope with four pedals (brake, reverse, valve cutoff, and fuel pressure). By 1905, sophistication extended to a free-engine clutch giving a neutral for traffic, and a two-speed rear axle, regarded similarly to the 'low' position on a modern automatic and reserved for exceptionally steep gradients.

White Steamers were the official transport of the White House in 1908. Here President Theodore Roosevelt takes the air in a 30 hp touring car.

Unfortunately, the gasoline revolution was under way. White sales reached their peak in 1906, and though they stayed over 1,000 units a year in ensuing seasons, from 1910 the company switched to petrol-engined luxury cars. After 1918 they abdicated into trucks, which they still make.

The White chassis was almost conventional in so far as the engine lived under a frontal bonnet, with the condenser taking the place of a petrol car's radiator. The underseat location of the boiler, however, alarmed nervous passengers.

Maxwell Model-L

1906, United States

Jonathan Maxwell had worked with the pioneer Haynes-Apperson concern in Indiana, and thus rated as a second-generation manufacturer. Also second-generation in outlook were his cars, still with horizontal engines, but now featuring shaft drive. Two cylinders replaced the solitary 'pot' of Oldsmobiles and Cadillacs, and the frontal bonnet was no dummy: it wore a Mercedes-style cooler for the thermo-siphon circulation. Inlet valves were mechanically-operated, though the old planetary transmission survived: it would be used on twin-cylinder Maxwells to the end of the line in 1912. The channel-section frame and semi-elliptic springing likewise reflected big-car practice, though Model-L still weighed in at around 1,000 lb (453 kg). It was also cheap: $780 in America, and 165 guineas in England, where it took its first bow in 1906. Top speed was 35 mph (56 km/h), and catalogues boasted of the 6 mph (9.5 km/h) available in reverse!

Maxwell sales passed the 2,000 mark for the first time that season, less than two years after the make's debut. The advent of a companion four-cylinder model led to the opening of a new factory at Newcastle, Indiana. In 1910 Maxwell joined the United States Motor Company, a consortium intended to rival William C. Durant's infant General Motors, its products embracing the inexpensive single-cylinder Brush as well as luxury models (Columbia, Stoddard-Dayton) and trucks (Alden-Sampson). But though 16,000 Maxwells were sold in 1911, the under-capitalized empire was riding for a fall, and in the ensuing bankruptcy only Maxwell lived to fight again. A line of cheap, conventional fours would carry them through to 1925, though the name barely survived a takeover by Walter P. Chrysler. The Maxwell's successors were the 50-series Chrysler (1925–28) and thereafter the Plymouth.

Hispano-Suiza 40/50 hp

1907, Spain

Poor, politically unstable, and ill-served with roads – the city of Cadiz was still approached by 'seas of mud and ruts' – Spain offered even less promise for motor manufacturers than did Italy. What she did possess was a youthful monarch, Alfonso XIII, who drove himself, and drove fast. Thus royal patronage was accorded to the Hispano-Suiza within a year of the make's inception.

As the name implied, the *marque*'s chief engineer was a Swiss from Geneva, Marc Birkigt, who arrived in Barcelona in 1899. Initially he worked in civil engineering, and then with Emilio La Cuadra's electric-car venture. Petrol-engined prototypes were also made before the money ran out: the same fate attended Birkigt's second backer, a certain Señor Castro, though in the two years of that company's life some advanced four-cylinder machinery with shaft drive and mechanically-operated side-valves in a T-head had been produced.

With healthier finances and the support of Damien Mateu, the Hispano-Suiza firm came into being in June 1904. Over the next two years Birkigt evolved further four-cylinder types based on the defunct Castro. Honeycomb radiators featured, ignition was by high-tension magneto, and Birkigt's gearboxes (like Henry Royce's) had four forward speeds with an overdrive top. The Swiss engineer was also a devotee of the unit box integral with the engine, soon to be general practice. Interestingly, the object of this exercise was not so much simplified production as structural strength. By using the box as a frame member he could cut down on cross bracing.

By 1907, the cars were becoming known outside Spain, with agencies in France and Britain. The 40/50 was a big car of 7.4 litres' capacity, with dual ignition and two plugs per cylinder, capable of 60mph (100km/h). For those demanding still more performance and flexibility there was a huge 11.2-litre six on a 128-inch (3.25m) wheelbase. Better still, royal patronage led to the development of a line of sports cars, and to successful participation in racing. The long-stroke 3.6-litre Alfonso model existed in prototype form in 1907, though the illustrious label itself arrived two years later, when Queen Victoria Eugenie gave her husband a white roadster as a birthday present.

The Hispano-Suiza badge combined the red-and-yellow of Spain with the white cross of designer Birkigt's native Switzerland.

1907 Hispano-Suiza 40/50hp

Rolls-Royce 40/50 hp

1907, Great Britain

At the beginning of 1907 Charles Stewart Rolls was better known than Frederick Henry Royce—he had, after all, won the previous year's Tourist Trophy on a 20hp Rolls-Royce. The factory was still in Manchester, and total deliveries to date amounted to less than 100 cars, with two, three, four, six and eight cylinders. Of these, the vee-eight was still-born, and the six-cylinder 30 notorious for crankshaft vibration.

Within three years, the *marque* had become a household word in luxury-car circles. The Silver Ghost might possess few revolutionary features. Other breeds (Austro-Daimler, the bigger Hotchkisses) might outpace it. What was recognized was that the six-cylinder 40/50, now the firm's staple product, gave an entirely adequate performance, gave it in smoothness and silence, and would go on giving it after mileages which left rival breeds ripe for the scrap-heap.

The fact that the original Silver Ghost (the name would be applied retrospectively to all side-valve 40/50s) had successfully undergone an officially observed 15,000-mile (24-000-km) trial was significant enough. Troubles were limited to a magneto failure (of little import with dual ignition) and one accidental closure of the petrol tap, and the car averaged 17.8mpg (16lit/100) as well as 2,500 miles (4,000km) per tyre. Little over £2 ($10) was needed to restore the vehicle to new condition at the end.

Royce was a perfectionist rather than an innovator. The main design features—side valves in an L-head, high-tension magneto ignition, cone clutch, four-speed sliding-type gearbox and bevel drive—were all well established, though few other makers as yet used full-pressure lubrication, dispensing with the messy sight-feeds. Exhaust pressure fuel feed was of course used on the 1901 Mercedes.

The 40–50 changed relatively little during a long run that ended in 1925. Inevitably the car received the 'period' refinements—quick-detachable wheels, electric lights and starter, and eventually four-wheel brakes—but major revision was confined to suspension and gearbox, apart from the elimination of the foot-operated transmission brake in 1913. Early cars had a supplementary transverse spring at the rear to eliminate side-sway with towering limousine bodies, this system giving way in due course to longitudinal cantilevers of Lanchester type. In 1909, the demand for silence would kill off the overdrive fourth gear, which offered effortless and surprisingly frugal cruising at 60mph (100km/h) at the price of an irritating whine. At the same time capacity went up to 7.4 litres.

None the less, even the early Ghosts were remarkable cars. A speed of 70mph was attainable with suitably light bodywork, a gallon of petrol lasted 16–18 miles, and a tourer could be bought complete for as little as £1,400 ($7,000), a lot of money compared with £200 runabouts in the de Dion or Rover class, but cheap in relation to foreign imports like the big Benz, Italas, and Lorraine-Dietrichs.

◄*Rolls-Royce's emblem was red, and would not change to black until 1933.*

A delightfully formal single cabriolet Rolls-Royce built by Barker on a 1912 chassis.

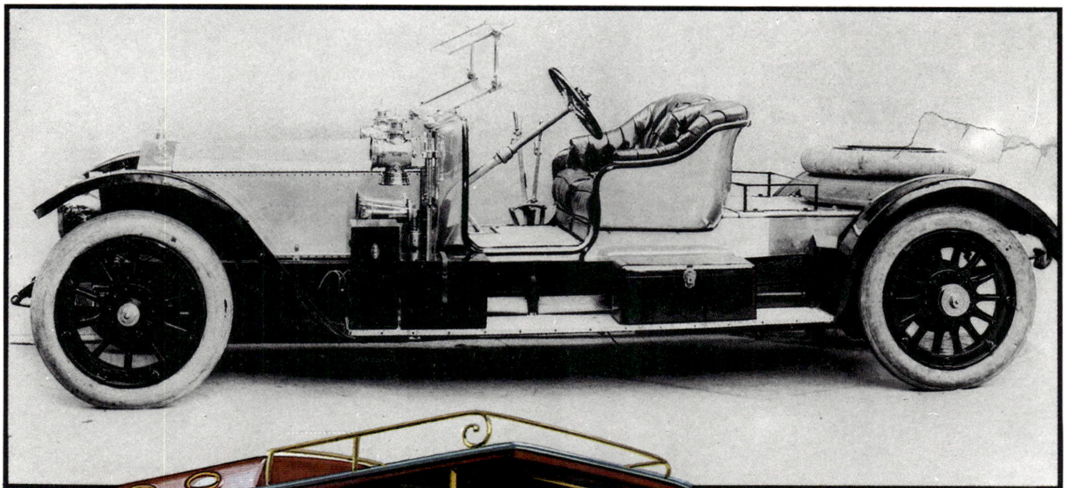

▲*Not all Rolls-Royce were intended for chauffeur-drive: Barker built this two-seater raceabout in 1909 or 1910. Note the two spare tyres on the rear deck.*

1907 Rolls-Royce 40/50 hp

The name 'Silver Ghost' is today applied to all 40/50 hp side-valve Rolls-Royce cars, but the car illustrated here is the true Silver Ghost. It was used for the legendary 15,000-mile RAC-observed trial in 1907, and preserved by its makers to this day. It is shown here outside Castle Malwood, the Hampshire home of its last private owner, Dan Hanbury.

The earliest Standards wore this simple badge, not the later Union Jack emblem with which the make is always associated.

1907 Standard 20 hp

Standard 20 hp

1907, Great Britain

1908 was perhaps the six-cylinder's first banner year, with no fewer than 55 different makes sold on the British market. Not all were large and expensive: the Standard illustrated here, for instance, rode on a compact 116-inch (2.95 m) wheelbase, with a capacity of a mere 3.3 litres as against the 12.9 of the biggest Itala. Better still, it offered a speed range of 2–40 mph (3–60 km/h) in direct drive ('without touching the clutch') for a modest £470 ($2,350). In this price bracket the customer would expect some vibration: the Standard cannot have been too gross an offender, for while many firms soon reverted to fours, its makers had a six continuously in their catalogue from 1905 to 1912.

Their sales were certainly helped by London agent Charles Friswell, who arranged for the despatch of a fleet of 20 hp cars to India in 1911 as official transport at King George V's Delhi Durbar. Nor were all these Standards small cars: while the 1907–8 model had originally been planned as a 1.9-litre to sell for under £300 ($1,500), at the other end of the scale was a huge 11½-litre 50 which made a brief appearance in 1907.

Engineering was conventional, though there were experiments with twin carburetters and air cooling in 1906, and some models had four-speed overdrive gearboxes. Frames were of pressed steel, inswept at the front and upswept at the rear, while the twin camshafts of early types had given way to the L-head configuration. Ignition was by magneto, and power was transmitted via a wet-plate clutch to a three-speed box. A recent innovation was Standard's shouldered radiator shell: this, and the Union Jack badge, would be hallmarks of the breed until 1930.

Turcat-Méry Six-Wheeler

1907, France

'Colonial' models engaged many a maker's attentions. These were recognizable by their bigger wheels, stiffer springs, and raised ground clearance. A more enterprising solution—subsequently applied to military vehicles—was the provision of extra wheels to take the load. This was pursued by Turcat-Méry of Marseilles, who designed cars for Lorraine-Dietrich, and built similar vehicles under their own name.

The vehicle illustrated is the Lorraine-Dietrich version, using the mechanical elements of their 40 hp chain-drive luxury tourer. To this was added an extra dead axle, the four rear wheels being interconnected by pairs of C-springs in series. The centre pair of wheels drove, while additional manoeuvrability was ensured by making the rearmost axle a steerer. This arrangement permitted the six-wheeler to surmount ditches, or even 12-inch logs.

The result was, however, far too unwieldy for a private car. In any case, a puncture-conscious public wanted no part of it: there were too many tyres to change. The idea never caught on, though a demonstrator came to London in 1907, and a magnificent berline was sold to the Khedive of Egypt. A truck version also appeared in that year's French Army vehicle trials.

Six-wheeled private cars like the Turcat-Méry have never caught on, largely because other and better means of smoothing the ride were achieved. Crossley and Morris-Commercial, however, toyed with machines for off-road use in 1928–31, some going to Indian princes as hunting cars.

OTAV $5\frac{1}{2}$hp
1908, Italy

The OTAV of 1908 anticipated the cyclecar boom by some three years. It also ran against the trend of Italian design, since Max Türkheimer, the Milanese cycle maker who backed it, hoped to find a market for a cheap runabout costing a mere one-seventh as much as full-size cars.

The chassis was conventional, apart from the use of quarter-elliptic springs (a recognized money-saver) all round. Front and rear axles were tubular, but the chain-cum-belt drive was far out-of-date, although the use of twin side belts for the final stage marked a reversal of the traditional Benz practice. A simple planetary gear gave two forward speeds, selected by a right-hand lever: no reverse was fitted since this was not required by law in Italy on 200-kilogram lightweights. Equally archaic was the engine, an aircooled single with automatic inlet valve. The 30 mph (50 km/h) top speed sounds possible, but on Italy's mountainous roads it can never have been the top-gear car it was alleged to be.

More sophisticated small cars were on their way. The OTAV had little export appeal even at bargain prices, and an economic crisis at home was playing havoc with market and industry alike. The make lasted only a year: even a merger with Giovanni Ceirano's Junior (a full size machine) could not save it. Italy would not offer a successful cheap baby car until the advent of the 990 cc Fiat 509 in 1924.

The OTAV might be underpowered for Italy and too primitive for most export markets, but in a British trial this example averaged more than 18 mph (29 km/h) and returned 38 mpg (7.5 lit/100).

1908 OTAV $5\frac{1}{2}$hp

A Renault completely equipped with hood, windscreen and lamps, though on this car only oil sidelamps are furnished, and there are no doors. The large number of these cars still running attests to their reliability.

Renault 8 hp

1908, France

In 1908, twin-cylinder cars still had a following in the 1-litre class. Right up to World War I a sizable proportion of Renault's output (4,600 units in 1908, over 10,000 in 1913) consisted of their excellent and dependable little twins. There was nothing cyclecar in their make-up: the side-valve engine was half a four, with Renault's proven thermo-siphon cooling and dashboard radiator, the latter doubling as a cockpit heater in winter. Ignition was by high-tension magneto, and the three-speed unit gearbox incorporated a direct top. The clutch was an inverted cone.

The car came in two wheelbase lengths, the longer being well-suited for taxicab work. The legendary *Taxis de la Marne*, in which General Galliéni rushed his troops from Paris to repel von Kluck's armies in 1914, were twin-cylinder Renaults. Top speed was an adequate 35 mph (56 km/h), and the Renault would plod happily along for hours on end at 25–30 mph (40–50 km/h). The only real fault was the progressive gearchange, hard to operate quietly, and retained to the end despite the standardization of the selective gate on other makes. Brakes were the usual rear-wheel and transmission type.

Initially, of course, Renault supplied chassis only, but during 1908 they made a bid in the cheap runabout market with the AX, illustrated above, on an 82½-inch (2.1 m) wheelbase frame and selling in England for £200 ($1,000) complete. 'Complete' was, of course, a relative term. There were no doors, and lamps and hood were extra!

Thomas Flyer 50 hp

1908, United States

From 1904 American industry concentrated more and more on bigger cars. These were constructed on European lines, and often designed by European engineers, too. Gustave Chedru from Clément-Bayard, and M. A. Longeron and Charles Muller (from Mors) worked for Thomas.

Erwin Ross Thomas had started as a bicycle manufacturer in Cleveland, Ohio. From there he moved to Buffalo, where he built motorcycles and light runabouts. The latter differed from other 'gas buggies' in having three-speed sliding-type gearboxes. The company's first 'European' models were, curiously, vertical-threes, the four-cylinder line beginning in 1904 with a 40 hp credited with 4–60 mph (6–100 km/h) in top. This followed Mercedes lines, with pair-cast cylinders, side valves in a T-head, steel frame, and side-chain drive, though early examples had quadrant change, and magneto ignition was not adopted until 1906. By this time Thomas had delivered over 1,000 large cars. In 1907 they opened a branch factory in Detroit to build smaller shaft-drive fours. This did not prosper, and was soon sold to Chalmers.

In 1908 came the Thomas's victory in the New York-Paris Race, while the company was supplementing its fours with a line of sixes headed by the enormous 12.8-litre K6-70, guaranteed to do 72 mph (115 km/h). Thereafter Thomas slid quietly downhill: the factory was sold up in 1913, despite a claim that 6,000 of the 7,000 cars built to date were still running.

Vauxhall 20hp
1908, Great Britain

Even as late as 1925 Britain's Vauxhall proudly bore the slogan: 'The Car Superexcellent', and was rated among the world's finest fast tourers. Yet Laurence Pomeroy's first design was almost an accident of birth.

Although early Vauxhalls had only vestigial flutes confined to the bonnet top, by 1908 these had become an identifying feature. They were still to be seen as late as 1962.

The former marine-engine works' first cars had been single-sylinder 'gas buggies' in the American idiom, noted for their all-coil springing and the flutes on the bonnet top, transferred to the radiator on later vertical fours. There had been some curious experiments, such as an inline three with six forward speeds, and a powered hansom cab in which the driver sat above and behind his fare. Had chief engineer F. W. Hodges not gone on holiday in Egypt shortly before the Royal Automobile Club's 1908 2,000-Mile Trial, the 20 might never have happened.

Pomeroy's chassis was conventional enough, with its half-elliptic springs and transmission-cum-rear-wheel brakes (the make's Achilles' Heel in post 1918 days). Where he scored was in his engine, an advanced affair designed for high rates of rotation. It achieved its 38bhp at a then alarming 2,000rpm, thanks to efficient gas flow, full-pressure lubrication, and a robust five-bearing crankshaft. Cooling was by thermo-siphon, a cone clutch was used, and in the Trial the car was the best overall performer. It proved capable of 55mph (90km/h) with an overall thirst of 26mpg (10.8lit/100). By 1910, a direct development, the Prince Henry sports model, offered 60bhp, and 1914's 4-litre versions were good for 75–80mph (120–130km/h).

The Thomas in the 1908 New York–Paris Race, loaded to capacity and complete with searchlight in front of the driver. The photograph was taken in open countryside now covered by Greater Los Angeles.

1908 Thomas Flyer 50hp

Ford Model-T
1909, United States

The Universal Car's achievements still astonish, even 70 years after its introduction. Its overall sales record during an 18-year run (over 16 million units) has been beaten only by the Volkswagen Beetle–and this car took over 30 years to do it. It brought motoring to the masses, while its descendants, the TT commercial (1917) and the Fordson tractor (1916) had the same effect on trucking and mechanized agriculture respectively. At peak in 1923, annual production came close to the two million mark. It was the model that popularized left-hand steering in America, while the need to make still more Ts led to the introduction of the moving assembly line.

When it first appeared, no one had ventured a full four-seater with a four-cylinder engine at less than $1,000 (£200). Its detachable cylinder head, a prime aid to servicing, was distrusted by many engineers, Henry Royce included, since early gaskets did not seal well. Towards the end, of course, the Ford became a joke: two-speed planetary transmissions were outmoded by 1912 and peculiar to the breed by 1918, while the car's indifferent two-wheel brakes and archaic non-styling had no place amid the sophistication of 1927. The public wanted bright colours, not the unrelieved black affected by Ford for so many years. Even if parts could be bought in every country store, the 'Tin Lizzie' had had its day.

Not so in 1909. Already established as America's best-selling maker with a $500 (£100) runabout, Ford now offered still more for $850 (£170). The slow-turning 2.9-litre four-cylinder engine gave a speed of 40 mph (64 km/h). The combination of transverse-leaf springing and a high ground clearance made it ideal for countries with bad, or non-existent roads. Further, the three-pedal layout adopted was proof against any combination of ignorance and panic, since whichever pedal one trod upon, it would at least retard the car's progress. The wide gap between high and low

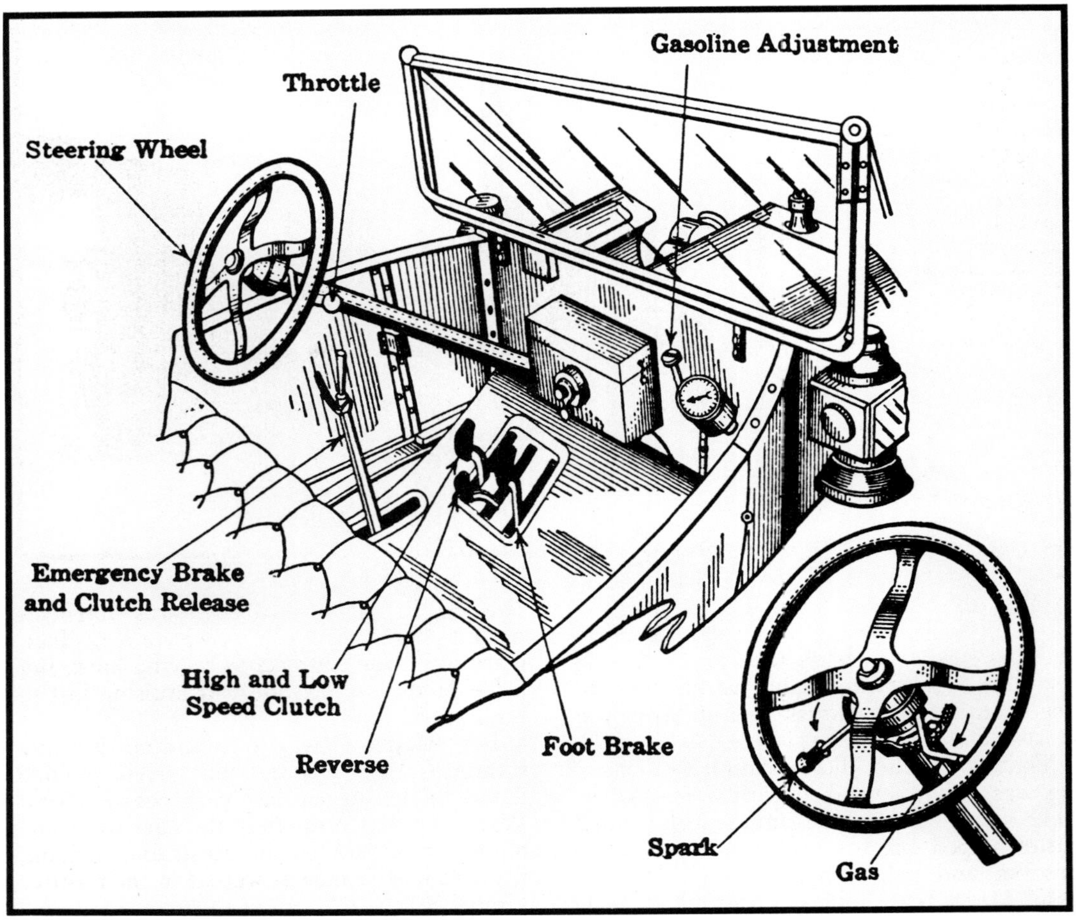

◄ *The foolproof motor-car at last, and the first car to popularize left-hand drive, if not its pioneer. The only lever is the handbrake; the three pedals, left to right, engaged low gear (which slowed the car effectively), reverse (the most dramatic method of stopping) and the footbrake (not very efficient). There were no instruments at all.*

► *The first Model-T touring cars were usually doorless. Front doors were not added until 1912.*

reduced the speed to 15 mph (24 km/h), the foot transmission brake did much the same, only less effectively, and the ultimate braking resource was reverse, also useful for the steepest hills (and on lesser ones when one was short of fuel!)

There were also idiosyncrasies. Cold starting was best undertaken with a rear wheel jacked up: otherwise gummed-up clutch plates helped one to crank the whole transmission, and risk being run over. Starters, available by 1919, were not compulsory until 1926. Another future delight was magneto-driven electric lighting: this gave a brilliant glare when the engine was revving hard, but a feeble glow when one was cruising fast in high gear.

But Model-T was outstanding by any standards. No wonder that over 300,000 found buyers in the last year before World War I, or that ultimately the cars would be made or assembled in Australia, Britain, Canada and France as well as in their native United States.

Martini's emblem commemorated the small arms with which the company made its name.

Martini 10hp
1909, Switzerland

Like the Vauxhall, Charles Baehni's 1909 Martini *voiturette* was an ancestor of the modern sports car. His miniature had been designed for the 1908 *Grand Prix des Voiturettes.* Once again we encounter a neat monobloc four-cylinder engine, albeit with only three main bearings and semi-pressure lubrication. Surprising at so early a date is the shaft-driven overhead camshaft, while fours are still uncommon in the 1,100cc class, where de Dion Bouton are content with one cylinder and Renault with two.

In other respects, the car is conventional enough, with magneto ignition, thermo-siphon cooling assisted by a vaned flywheel, and a pressed steel frame. A separate sub-chassis is retained for the engine and three-speed gearbox, and exhaust pressure feed is not usually found on light cars.

Switzerland was still no nation of motorists. As late as 1913, the country registered less than 5,000 private cars. Martini themselves had led a chequered career. Famed for their repeater rifle, they had made a petrol engine as early as 1887, and were experimenting with complete cars by 1897, though when deliveries began five years later, the product was a licence-built Rochet-Schneider, itself a copy of the Mercedes. From 1904 to 1906, the firm had been under British control. Though 1909 was a good year, with 260 cars sold, the sporting little overhead-camshaft two-seater was short-lived. By mid-1910 the advanced engine had given way to a 1.4-litre side-valve.

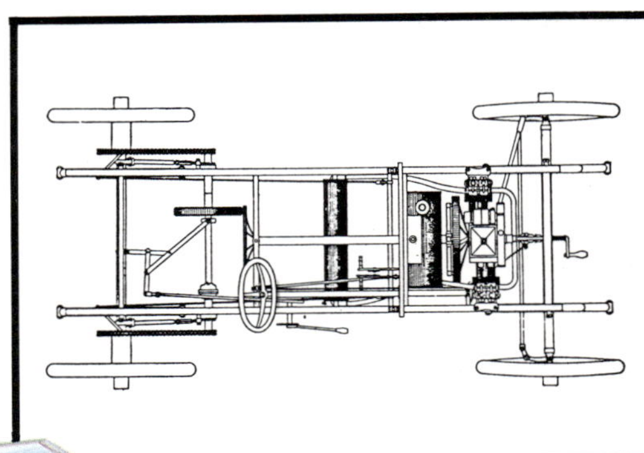

1909 Metz

The simple Metz chassis for do-it-yourself car builders. The aircooled engine lives at the front, with the fuel tank on the firewall in accordance with contemporary light-car practice. The transversely mounted silencer and exhaust pipe are less usual.

Metz
1909, United States

Those who regard the kit-car as a tax-dodging device of the 1950s and 1960s may be surprised to discover that an American firm sold no fewer than 6,000 such kits in the 1909–11 period. Under the Metz plan, the customer received his car in 14 successive packages. These started with frame elements and a set of tools, and ended with tank, carburetter, silencer, lamps, horn and starting handle. Each package cost $27 (£4.40), and terms were cash on the nail.

The idea was devised by Charles H. Metz to put the insolvent Waltham Manufacturing Company back on a paying basis. The scheme cleared the inventory of obsolete parts, and was self-financing. There were, of course, problems. Metz designed the car as he went along, and sometimes more adroit customers got ahead of him. Several of the later packages sold below cost, and though the scheme was launched in the summer of 1908, the first complete kits had not been delivered before October, 1909.

The specification embraced a 10hp aircooled flat-twin engine, an infinitely variable gear, full-elliptic springs, cycle-type wire wheels, bicycle-style brakes at the rear, and a stark two-seater body panelled in aluminium. No hood or windscreen was provided. By 1911 the fortunes of the company were safely restored, and Metz, encouraged by the success of his latest four-cylinder design in the Glidden Tour, offered this only in complete form, still with friction drive. Production reached its peak in 1915, with 7,230 Metzes delivered.

Sears Autobuggy
1909, United States

The short vogue of the high-wheeler was largely confined to America's Middle West. Between 1907 and 1912 perhaps 100,000 were built: at peak, in 1909, 41 different makes were on the market.

Here was a motorized buggy for the farmer, with piano box body, full-elliptic springs, and horse-carriage wheels of generous diameter with solid tyres. This not only resulted in good ground clearance and light weight (the latter important if one ditched the vehicle), but rendered manufacture simple. The vast buggy industry supplied all but the mechanical elements. These were a slow-turning aircooled flat-twin engine, and a simple friction or planetary drive. No more than two speeds were required, since hills were few and far between. Tiller steering was general practice. Such a vehicle was cheap: a 1909 Sears retailed for $395 (£79).

The celebrated Sears Roebuck mail order house accounted for some 3,500 units, all sold complete with 32-page instruction manual. A Sears, they said, would 'do anything that a $5,000 car will do, except travel faster than 25 miles an hour'. It was 'up with the chickens, knows no quitting time, and after a day's work is ready for a pleasure trip in the evening'. So, of course, was a Ford, backed by cheap parts and service, and twice as quick. Sears quietly dropped complete automobiles from their catalogues after 1912.

An aircooled car had no radiator to carry a badge, so Sears used old-fashioned brass script. Cars were a short-lived line for this nationally famous mail-order house.

1909 Sears Autobuggy

Sheffield-Simplex 45 hp

1909, Great Britain

By 1909 the automobile worked admirably: at least, expensive ones did. Owners with 'motor servants' need never bother themselves with the chores of polishing brass and keeping paint-and-varnish pristine. Tyres, of course, were still a cross to be borne, but the major remaining problem was shifting gears. And since synchromesh lay well in the future, the best palliative was a car that would do 90 per cent of its work in top.

Planetary transmissions were a partial cure, though on these 'low' was very low and still called for frequent use. Six-cylinder engines made for greater flexibility, but even with these most makers retained three- and four-speed gear-sets, just to be on the safe side. Not so Earl Fitzwilliam's Sheffield-Simplex company, which advertised a 45 hp 'gearboxless' car in 1909, with pictures of the prototype scaling the toughest passes of its native Yorkshire.

The company had acquired the rights of the four-cylinder Brotherhood car, after its makers had moved from London to Peterborough and lost interest in such activities. Thereafter, fours gave way to an elegant 7-litre six (its cylinder dimensions of 114.3 × 114.3 mm were identical to those of the 40–50 Rolls-Royce. There were other similarities, though Sheffield-Simplex did not use full-pressure lubrication, preferred three speeds to four, combined the footbrake and clutch, and used an accelerator pedal with lateral travel, which last must have confused not a few drivers! The round radiator was a distinguishing feature, and a tourer cost only £855 ($4,275).

The 'gearboxless' 45 (Type LA2) was not, of course, a one-gear car. Instead, the conventional arrangements gave way to a two-speed transaxle alleged to save 150 parts and 300 lb (136 kg). Detachable wire wheels were standardized, and the car would, of course, 'climb anything in top'. Sheffield-Simplex had sufficient confidence in their product to furnish one for the Prince of Wales's West country tour. An officially observed trial showed a 3–60 mph (5–100 km/h) range in top, while use of low when accelerating from rest to 30 mph (50 km/h) saved less than half a second. But though the transaxle survived on Sheffield-Simplexes to the end of production in 1915, 1913 and later models all came with three speeds. And also, be it said, with orthodox accelerator pedals!

The entwined 'S' badge of Sheffield-Simplex took a leaf out of Rolls-Royce's book. The company also conducted a formidable testing programme in Scotland and the Pennines.

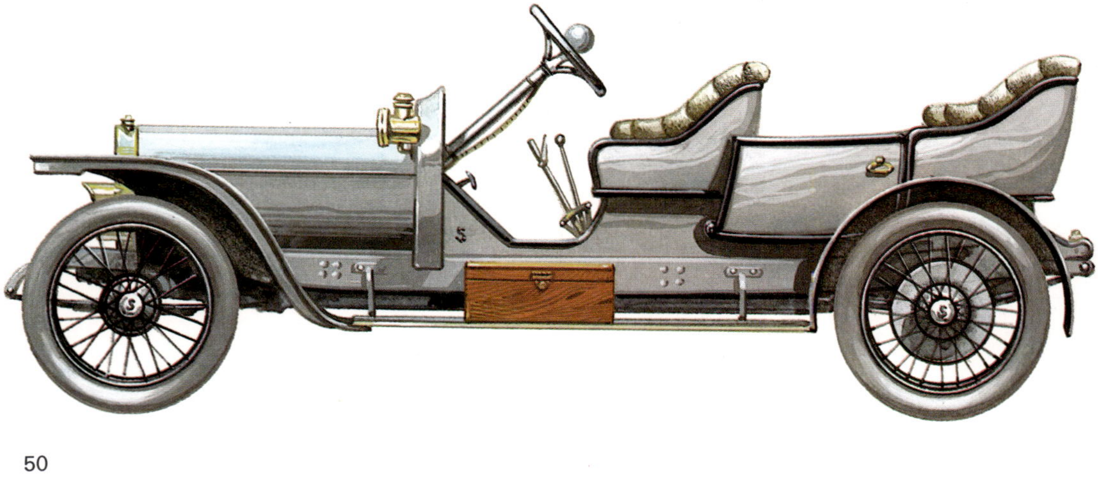

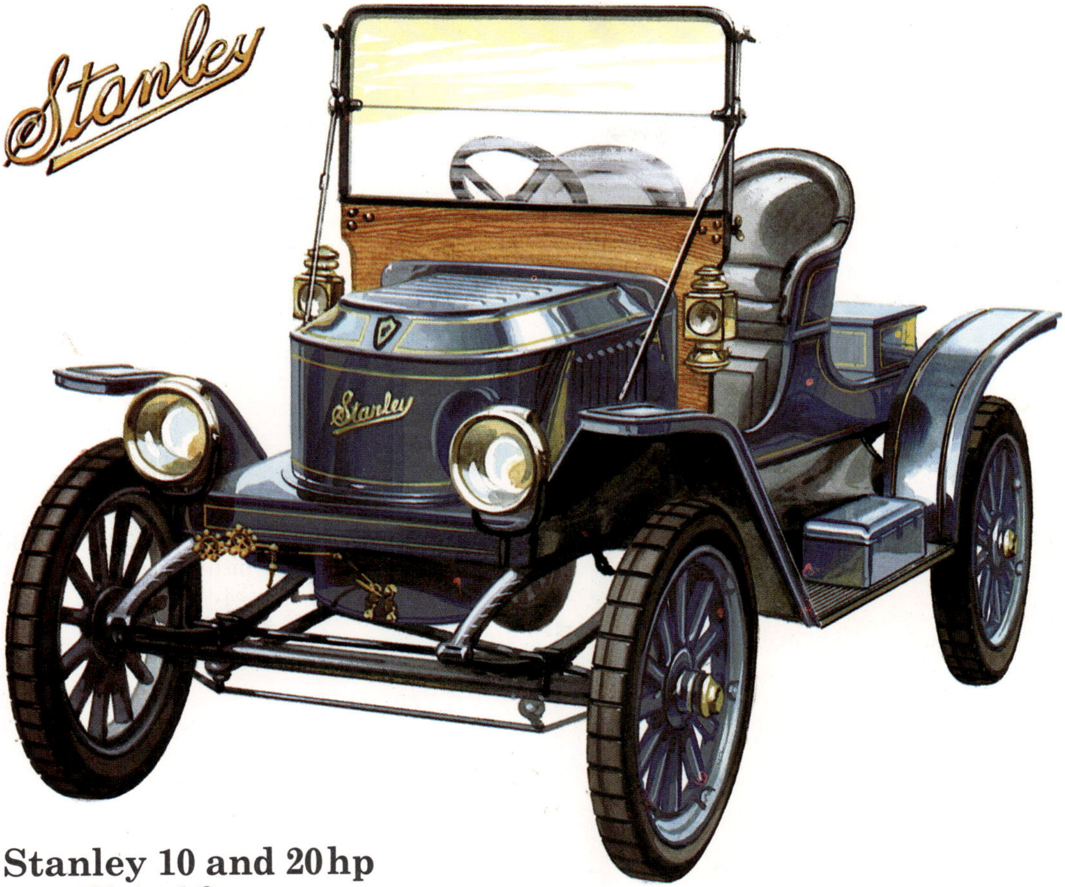

Stanley 10 and 20 hp

1909, United States

If White and other steam-car makers (such as Miesse in Belgium) were deserting their first love, the Stanley brothers, back in control of their company since 1902, were irrevocably wedded to the system. Stanley steam cars would be made until 1926, though their 1909 offering was now outwardly conventional, apart from the coffin nose housing the vertical, multi-tubular boiler. Unlike Whites, Stanleys had no condenser, in spite of which the 26-gallon (130-litre) water tank gave a useful range of 50 miles (80 km).

Simplicity remained the keynote. The car's double-acting, simple, twin-horizontal cylinder engine was mounted at the rear with the crankshaft engaging directly on the differential, eliminating the complexities of gears or chains. Steering was of course by wheel, and the wooden chassis rode on full-elliptic springs. The footbrake incorporated a ratchet for parking, while the provision of oil-bath lubrication for the engine simplified maintenance still further.

A paraffin burner was now used, a great improvement on the infuriating firing-iron of Locomobile days, and acetylene lighting systems such as the Prestolite could be adapted to preheat the vaporizer. But there was still the problem of the 25–30 minutes needed to raise steam from dead cold, even if the steam car's habits were essentially more predictable than those of internal-combustion types. The silence of a Stanley engine was offset by an irritating whistle from the burner.

As for the neck snapping acceleration, this was undoubtedly available. Frank Marriott had, after all, attained 127.66 mph (204.25 km/h) at Daytona Beach in 1906 in a Stanley racer, and the cars could be 'rodded' by putting a big-capacity 20 hp boiler in the short '10 hp' chassis. A Stanley was good for 50 mph (80 km/h) and could get there far faster than any stock petrol car, but after a short burst one ran out of steam. The comfortable cruising speed remained 30 mph (50 km/h).

Napier 45 hp
1910, Great Britain

In the first decade of the 20th century, the Napier was certainly the most respected British make. The 'first to wear the green' and represent their country in international racing, they had won the 1902 Gordon Bennett Cup. When Germany and France shared the technical leadership between them, Napier – even if they had not invented the six-cylinder engine – could legitimately claim that they were the most consistent of its protagonists, marketing the type without a break, the war years apart, from 1904 to 1924. (Their great publicist S. F. Edge made immense capital out of this.)

A six-cylinder Napier took the world's first 24-hour record at Brooklands in 1907, and Edge never missed out on any stunt that might enhance the car's reputation. As early as 1906, a 60 was submitted to a 1,000-mile (1,600 km) observed top-gear trial, and in 1910 Arthur Macdonald drove a six-cylinder car from London to Edinburgh without a downward shift, turning in 19.35 mpg (14.7 lit/100). Britain's prevailing 20 mph (32 km/h) limit precluded any mention of his average speed, but he subsequently did a Brooklands lap at 76.35 mph (122.18 km/h) leaving the Napier's performance in no doubt. Napiers were made under licence in Italy; American manufacture was also planned, but scarcely began.

The catalogued six-cylinder range of 1910 featured pair-cast, L-head engines with pump and fan cooling and dual ignition. Fuel feed was by exhaust pressure from a rear tank, and the semi-elliptic rear suspension was supplemented by a transverse leaf spring. Standard wheelbase was 134 inches (3.42 m), this chassis coming with two sizes of engine, the 6.2-litre 45 and the 9.7 litre 60; an even larger 90 hp unit was also available. Wire wheels were usually fitted, and the breed's distinguishing features were the forward mounted radiator and its tall 'water tower' filler cap. The smaller 45 was good for over 60 mph (100 km/h), and Edge shrugged the roughness of the unbalanced crankshaft away as the 'power rattle'.

Though Napier finally abdicated from

Napier's first six-cylinder racing car, built in 1904, is here seen contesting the 1905 British Gordon Bennett eliminating trials. It did not do well in the race, however, as its two-speed gearbox could not cope with the steep gradients of the course.

A Napier for a Maharajah, with an engine rated at 120 hp. The extended chassis gave a length of 21 feet (6.5m), and there was room for 11 passengers.

1910 Napier 45hp

The front end of a 1914 Napier, showing the make's tall 'water tower' radiator cap.

racing in 1908, sales remained good, reaching a peak in 1911 with 801 cars delivered. The company, however, suffered (like Daimler in later years) from a divided image. Edge might seek to promote the big and luxurious sixes, so much so that his 1908 Tourist Trophy fours were badged and entered as Huttons – but the factory's bread-and-butter came from smaller fours and, worse still, from twin-cylinder taxicabs, a profitable line for several years. (Between 1909 and 1913 nearly 1,500 cabs left the Acton works.) Moreover, well-heeled clients did not like the sight of that aristocratic water-tower on the cabs they hailed in Pall Mall. Edge's resignation in 1913 took much of the fire out of the publicity side, and though a one-model policy (with an ohc six) was pursued after 1918, by this time Napier were pinning their faith solely on aero engines. The last cars were delivered in 1924.

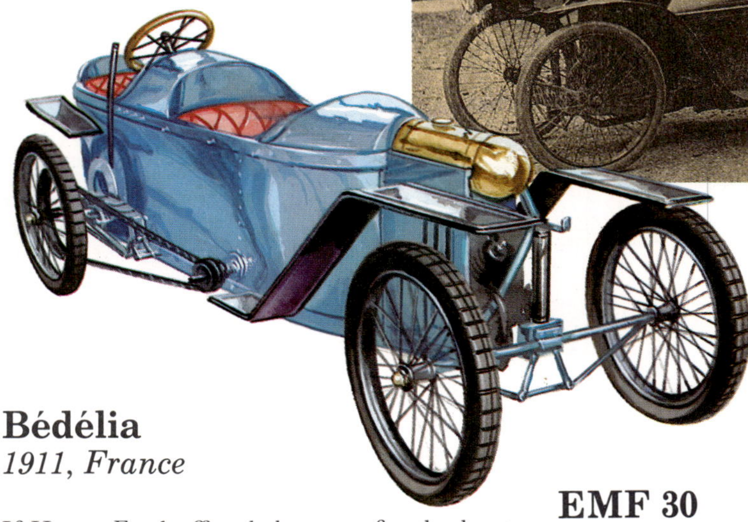

A Bédélia in full road trim. With the narrow track, there was room for only a single headlight, and the windscreen was so far away from the driver that he had to wear goggles. The car was hardly wide (or robust) enough for two passengers, either.

Bédélia
1911, France

If Henry Ford offered the most for the least money, it could be said of the cyclecar that at best it offered sociable accommodation for one graduate motor-cyclist and a friend, while at worst it presented the maximum degree of discomfort the customer could be persuaded to accept.

The French Bédélia was not even sociable: its crew sat in tandem, with the driver behind, as on an 1896 Bollée. The main structure consisted of four ash longerons, with aluminium side panels and a wooden floor. Wheels were of cycle type, and the vehicle combined a centre-pivoting front axle with cable-and-bobbin steering. Engines were of aircooled motor-cycle type: either a proprietary single by Quentin or Bédélia's own vee-twin with automatic inlet valves. In the best motor-cycle tradition, the fuel tank lived atop this unit. The transmission likewise recalled the Bollée: a primary belt to the mainshaft, whence the power was delivered to the wheels by two long side belts. There was no differential, and 'gears' were changed by slackening the motor lugs to move the axle forward in relation to the transmission.

The Bédélia had one major asset: it was very light–335 lb (150 kg) with the twin-cylinder engine. It could also be bought for less than £50 ($250) in France, though the lowest figure quoted in England was £62 ($310), raised to £94 ($470) by the end of 1911, when both 50 mph (80 km/h) and 50 mpg (5.5 lit/100) were claimed. Remarkably, the cars were still available in 1925, though by this time tandem seating had been abandoned.

EMF 30
1911, United States

One of the forerunners of the Studebaker, the EMF was marketed by that company, and made for them by Everitt-Metzger-Flanders. A cut above Ford and Overland, it sold in the $1,100–1,250 (£220–250) bracket: the same factory's humbler Flanders cost $800 (£160).

In this price class, even in 1909, one expected a proper three-speed, sliding-type gearbox, though the makers mounted it in unit with the back axle, never a very healthy idea. For the rest, the car was orthodox, with a pair-cast four-cylinder engine, magneto ignition, splash lubrication, and cone clutch. The full-elliptic rear springs were designed to cope with America's bad roads, while no transmission brake was fitted: Americans disliked them. The fixed wood wheels wore demountable rims, and the standard colour was blue, with cream running gear.

On paper, the EMF's 50 mph (80 km/h) top speed and 22 mpg (12.5 lit/100) sounded attractive for a 3.7-litre car, but it was dogged by trouble. The first thermo-siphon cooled engines boiled furiously, so a pump was hurriedly substituted. The unreliability of the transaxle earned the car such sobriquets as 'Every Mechanical Fault' and 'Every Morning Fix It'. In spite of this, the combined EMF and Flanders sales climbed steadily, from 7,960 in 1909 to a peak of just over 29,000 in 1912.

For 1913 the EMF and Flanders names were dropped, and the range marketed as Studebakers. The transaxle, however, had several more years to run.

1911 EMF 30

Métallurgique 26 hp
1911, Belgium

When fitted with coachwork by Vanden Plas of Brussels, the Belgian Métallurgique was one of the most beautiful cars of its period. There were such creations as a chariot-style limousine with imitation venetian blinds to the rear quarters, and a 'lounge saloon' for the owner driver with interior electric light. One closed car was given the full Louis XVI treatment, down to Venetian lace headrests and a cupola-style roof. The elegance was completed by the rounded-vee radiator, which set the fashion for a whole generation of sporting cars in Germany. The influence was not surprising: Métallurgiques were designed by a German, Ernst Lehmann, and they were also made under licence in Berlin by Bergmann.

This beauty was more than skin-deep, for Métallurgiques had a well-substantiated reputation for performance. In 1908 their 60/80 hp four (they never made a six) with overhead inlet valves disposed of 86 bhp, and though the side-valve models were less spectacular, the 26, illustrated below, was no sluggard, doing 80 mph (128 km/h) in open form on an output of 60 bhp from 4.9 litres. Specification was close to the period's norm, with pair-cast cylinders, side valves in an L-head, and magneto ignition. The gearbox offered four speeds, and rear springs were three-quarter elliptic. Wire wheels and polished aluminium bonnets were standard equipment, and by 1914 Métallurgique sold their chassis with a two-year guarantee.

War damage and the gradual failure of the all-important British market, however, took their toll, and these former makers of railway equipment built their last car in 1927.

The Métallurgique in classic form, 1914: an interior-drive saloon body with low-pressure tyres to smooth the ride.

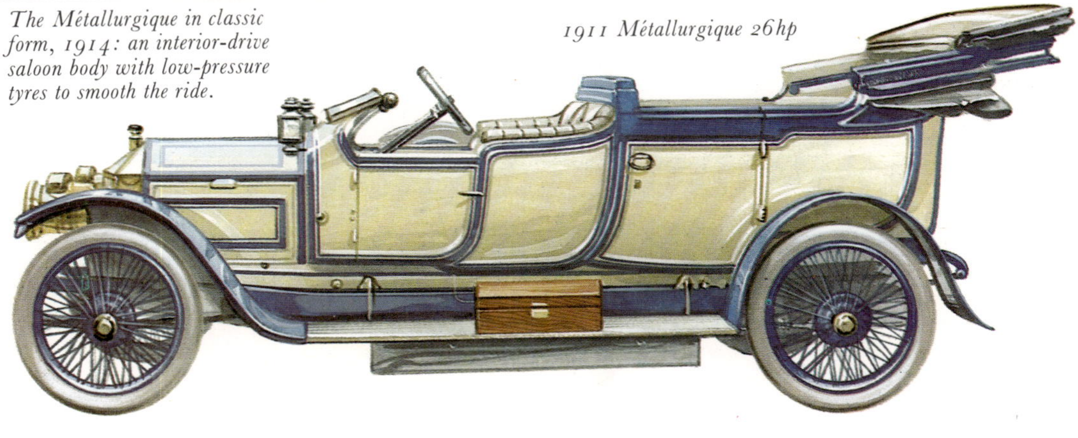

1911 Métallurgique 26hp

Stoewer B6

1911, Germany

Before 1914 local makes could survive on local sales – in the bigger countries. Of such a stamp was the Stoewer from Stettin in Pomerania, though Émile Mathis's Strasbourg-based agency introduced the breed to Western Germans; it also allowed Mathis to put his own badge on some Stoewers! Export sales were surprisingly good, accounting for some 50 per cent of total production, and extending as far afield as Australia. Annual production, however, seldom passed the 2,000 mark even in the prosperous mid-thirties.

The brothers Bernhard and Emil Stoewer started by making bicycles in the family ironworks, progressing to motor-cycles and tricycles of de Dion type by 1897. These were followed by chain-drive cars in the Panhard idiom (1901) and mock-Mercedes from 1902 onward. The imitative phase was, however, nearly over. Shaft-drive cars were first seen in 1904, and three years later chains had gone for good. In their place came some interesting and individual designs.

These were small fours of L-head monobloc configuration, modern for the period and an anticipation of what would be standard practice by 1914. Lubrication was of semi-pressure type, cooling was by thermo-siphon, and the Stoewers preferred wet-plate clutches. Detail specifications varied: there were three speeds on the smallest B1 and four speeds on larger versions, which also used exhaust pressure fuel feed instead of gravity. B1s, though not B6s, had three-quarter-elliptic rear springs designed for the poor road conditions in Eastern Europe.

A wide range was offered in 1911, from a diminutive $1\frac{1}{2}$-litre up to an enormous 8.8-litre six and a four-cylinder car with a Knight sleeve-valve engine purchased complete from Daimler of Coventry. The B6 was credited with 30 mpg (9.5 lit/100). Oil consumption, however, was in the region of 500 mpg (56 lit/100).

Delaunay-Belleville SMT

1912, France

With their round radiators as a reminder of their makers' origins – Delaunay-Belleville's marine boilers were world-famous – these cars were among the aristocrats of Edwardian motordom. One never drove a Delaunay – one was driven in it. Among those who favoured the breed were Indian princes, British peers, the President of the French Republic, the King of Greece and, above all, the last Tsar of All the Russias, whose garages contained 20 examples. His three flagships, delivered between 1909 and 1912, were the enormous SMTs. The designation stood for *Sa Majesté Le Tsar*, and the model was exclusive to him. No other crowned head could have one.

Even by Delaunay-Belleville's standards the cars were enormous – and their regular sixes were big enough. Top of the 1911 range was the 9.3-litre CA, and even in the 1914–20 period, when the age of monsters was over, there was still an 8-litre, the O-type, complete with twin transmission brakes, one at each end of the gearbox, and linked to twin pedals. The forward one was uncomfortably close to the flywheel, and caught fire easily. And while standard Delaunays no longer used chain drive, it was still found on the SMT. Wheelbase was 161 inches (4.08m), and the interior equipment included canteens, ashtrays and even matchboxes in solid silver, electric light and heaters. With that seven-bearing crankshaft of formidable length, one may hope that the car was never driven at high speeds.

If staid by reputation, the make was not devoid of advanced thinking. Even on the first four-cylinder cars, announced in 1904, full-pressure lubrication was used. Delaunays always featured comprehensive undershielding, and a Barbey compressed-air starter was a regular option. This could be employed to jack up the wheels, inflate the tyres, and blow a whistle. Monobloc engines were found on smaller Delaunays, magneto ignition was standard, and most models had four forward speeds. Electric lighting and demountable rims had made their appearance by 1913, and starters were available a year later. Medium-sized cars were not impossibly expensive: a 4.4-litre HB6 chassis cost £600 ($3,000) in England. Between 1908 and 1915 the firm turned out 3,754 of their sixes alone, an impressive record.

'One doesn't drive a Delaunay-Belleville – it simply isn't done.' So they said in France, and this advertisement stresses the need for a chauffeur.

Rover 12 hp

1912, Great Britain

In the years just prior to World War I the family car was taking shape. In Europe, there had of course been no such thing in the pioneer years, but with more dependable engineering came a flood of middle-class buyers. The British norm of 1912–15 can best be summarized as a '15.9 hp' according to the RAC taxation formula. This meant a capacity of between 2.3 and 2.8 litres, four cylinders, side valves, cone clutch, three- or four-speed gearbox, and bevel drive. Such a vehicle would cruise comfortably at 35 mph (56 km/h) and cost somewhere between £350 ($1,750) and £450 ($2,250). For this sum the client would expect hood, screen and detachable wheels, though he would also expect to pay extra for electric lighting. Starters were an unthinkable luxury before 1914.

Owen Clegg's Rover 12, new for 1912, came close to such parameters. True, cylinders of 75 mm bore made it a 14 for tax purposes, but this had little significance as long as taxation was low. Clegg considered three forward speeds sufficient; like Lanchester, he also preferred the quiet and durable worm-drive axle. A transmission brake was retained, and the cylinder head was non-detachable, but in other respects the side-valve monobloc engine was very modern, with integral manifolding, a carburetter bolted direct to the block, and even an oil dipstick, a real novelty for these days. Wheelbase was 110 inches (2.8 m), sufficient for roomy five-seater bodies, the steel wheels were detachable and electric lighting was part of his £350 ($1,850) package. With a top speed of 43 mph (69 km/h) the car would cruise at the desired velocity, while at 2,408 lb (just under 1,100 kg) it was not excessively heavy.

It also put the famous Coventry firm well and truly on the map. Rover had done fairly well in early days with their simple single-cylinder runabouts, and their 20 hp four had won the 1907 Tourist Trophy, but the singles had gone on too long, and a line of small sleeve-valve machinery had not helped. Clegg noted that the fours were the best-sellers, and scrapped the existing five-model range in favour of two such types, the 12 and a 3.3-litre 18.

By mid-1912, however, he had been seduced across the Channel by Darracq, also in trouble through involvement with 'valveless' engines, albeit of a different type. He rescued them with what amounted to a carbon copy of the Rover, but his work in England had been well done, and that company's 12 sold 1,943 units in 1914. In improved form with full electrics, it would be revived after the war, as a 14, and produced until 1924.

►*The front end of the Rover. Full integration of body and chassis is still a long way away, and there is no smooth line from firewall to bonnet. The mascot in this case is not Rover's traditional Viking. The electric lighting is worth noting: by 1915 the headlamps would be rigidly attached to the radiator—advanced practice for those days.*

▼ *The large-diameter wheels, comprehensive weather protection and high ground clearance identify this Rover as a 'Colonial' model, a regular addition to European makers' ranges in pre-1914 days. Not visible are the stiffer springs. Unusually, this car has acetylene lighting, with the generator on the running board.*

Hillman 9.5 hp

1913, Great Britain

By 1913, the big car in miniature was becoming popular: even America had one, in the shape of the Saxon (opposite). Typical of the British idiom, if perhaps less common than Morris, Singer or Standard, was A. J. Dawson's 9.5 hp Hillman, of which 450 were sold in 1914.

The 1.4-litre L-head monobloc engine had a two-bearing crankshaft, magneto ignition, and gravity feed from a tank on the streamlined dash. The usual cone clutch and three-speed gearbox transmitted the power to an overhead worm back axle, springs were semi-elliptic and wheels of steel detachable type. For £200 ($1,000) one got a hood, windscreen, number plates, tools and spare wheel complete with tyre; only the side and tail lamps (and, curiously, the horn) were electrified. The Hillman would put 25 miles (40 km) into the hour under normal road conditions, and return 30–35 mpg (8–9.4 lit/100).

Competition was fierce: in 1914 the Hillman had eight direct native rivals, from AC to Standard, plus two from France (Clément-Bayard and de Dion-Bouton) and the Mathis from Germany. Cheapest of the lot was the Humberette, but its vee-twin engine put it in the cyclecar class despite its conventional driveline. Hillman could not compete against Calthorpe and Morris, with respective prices of £168 ($840) and £175 ($875). Thus for 1915 the company moved up a class with a 102-inch (2.59 m) wheelbase, 1.6-litre engine, and full electrics, including a starter. This 11 hp would form the basis for post-war production.

Hillman's badge symbolized the three spires of Coventry cathedral, still recognizable in this pre-1914 version.

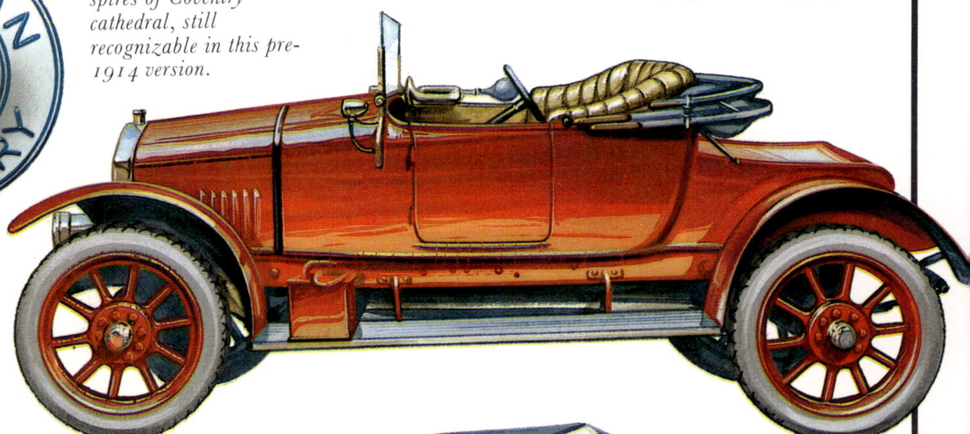

1913 Hillman 9.5 hp

1913 National 40

1913 Saxon Four

National 40
1913, United States

Just before World War I America was making splendid, if spartan sports cars like Mercer, Stutz, and the huge chain-drive Simplex. This was a logical aspect of standardization. With stereotyped automobiles being turned out in vast quantities, there were customers who wanted something different, and were prepared to pay over $2,000 (£400) for it.

Highly respected was the National from Indianapolis, product of a firm which had tried air cooling and battery-electric cars in its time; it would fade out with an abortive light plane in the mid-30s. National's 1913 offering was a curious mixture of ancient and modern.

Under the bonnet was a hefty pair-cast four of the old T-head configuration, with air-pressure feed from a big rear tank, and dual ignition with two sets of spark plugs. Wheels were fixed, with demountable rims, but there was no transmission brake. Three forward speeds sufficed: controls were standard American, with left-hand steering and central change. Electric lights and an electric starter were inclusive at the list price of $3,150 (£630), while an interesting refinement was the engine-driven tyre pump, a boon when inflating those big 36-inch tyres!

National's 1913 catalogue claimed 187 firsts, 114 seconds and 79 third places in recent competitions. 'Race victories', they said, 'do not stop at the end of the race. They live forever in the character of the car and the way it is built'.

Saxon Four
1913, United States

America had a brief cyclecar craze, though the conventional small car was rare in a land of low taxes and cheap fuel. The successful Saxon was, however, European in capacity and dimensions. Its $1\frac{1}{2}$-litre four-cylinder Continental engine was essentially the same as that fitted to 1915–19 Morris-Cowleys; wheelbase was a modest 96 inches (2.438 m); weight was only 1,150 lb (525 kg); and it was offered only as a two-seater. The factory's claims included 35 mpg (8 lit/100) and 200 miles to the *quart* of oil, a sad commentary on the unfrugal habits of splash systems! Tyre consumption was said to be low.

The simple side-valve engine was cooled by thermo-siphon. Coil ignition was preferred to a magneto, and for the $395 (£79) asked in 1913 the customer got neither electrics nor instruments. Windscreen and tool kit were, however, included, and the cycle-type wire wheels soon gave way to the usual wood artilleries. To save money, Saxons made do with a two-speed transaxle, gear change was of the outmoded quadrant type, and springs were quarter-elliptic. With an eye on export markets, right-hand drive was available, and quite a few Saxons reached Britain, especially during the wartime American car boom of 1915–16. Over 30,000 of the original fours were turned out before the company switched, perhaps unwisely, to a small six in 1917.

Despite the adoption of assembly-line production, modest prices and a switch back to fours in 1920, the company folded in 1922.

The Maltese Cross badge of Crossley cars.

Crossley 25/30 hp tenders for the Royal Flying Corps being delivered in 1915. They have special wide rear wheel rims and dual tyres.

Crossley 25/30 hp

1914, Great Britain

To British servicemen in World War I, the 25/30 Crossley was the equivalent of the Humber Super Snipe of 1939/45 – a military maid of all work. It served as a staff car, ambulance, and, first and foremost, as the Royal Flying Corps's standard tender. Even after this Service became the Royal Air Force in 1918, the 'RFC' label clung to the car.

The Crossley was an odd case of technical regression. When first introduced for 1910, it had uncoupled four-wheel brakes, but these (unlike Argyll's more effective system) proved skid-prone and were dropped after a couple of seasons, leaving the 25/30 (and subsequent large four-cylinder Crossleys) to sit it out to the end on the old combination of a transmission footbrake and rear-wheel handbrake. The rest represented solid British engineering. The cylinders of the side-valve four-cylinder engine were cast in pairs, with semi-pressure lubrication, and a massive five-bearing crankshaft. Cooling was by thermo-siphon with fan assistance, the high-tension magneto was backed by a coil, and the ratios of the four-speed gearbox were selected by a right-hand lever. Tubular cross members were used in the frame, and wheels were detachable: special wide rims and twin rear tyres identified military models. The Crossley was good for 60 mph (100 km/h) and 17 mpg (16.5 lit/100); sports models, distinguished by their 'trout-nose' (rounded-vee) radiators, were appreciably faster, and did well in pre-war sprints. This vee radiator was standardized on all 25/30s from 1919 onward.

Having been in continuous production throughout the war, Crossley were among the first British makers to resume deliveries after the Armistice. The 25/30 became the correct form of prestige transport in the Empire: several were used on the Prince of Wales's tour of India in 1921, and he subsequently owned two cars of this type. Four went to the King of Siam in 1922, while a pair of tenders was used by Major Court-Treatt on his Cape-London voyage in 1924–5.

Delage Type-AK

1914, France

The small six is generally regarded as a phenomenon of the late twenties and early thirties; in any case, the type generally had fallen out of favour around 1910. But a demand for ultra-flexible cars compact enough for a woman to drive had led to models of less than 3 litres capacity, available in 1914 from Loreley in Germany, Hillman in England, and Delage in France. Louis Delage had started in 1905 with proprietary-engined singles, bludgeoning his way to fame by supporting races on a shoestring. He had been rewarded by victory in the 1907 *Coupe des Voiturettes* and between 1909 and 1914 he marketed some excellent $1\frac{1}{2}$-litre fours.

Outwardly this new AK type resembled an elongated four, with its neatly streamlined dash incorporating external petrol and oil filler caps. The engine, too, was a neat, side-valve monobloc affair with integrally-cast manifolds, magneto ignition, and full-pressure feed for the three-bearing (formerly four-bearing) crankshaft. The clutch was a cone, and a four-speed gearbox soon replaced the three-speed type. Already Delage had relegated his transmission brake to a back-up role: the pedal worked in drums on the rear wheels. The maximum output of 30 bhp was delivered at 2,000 rpm, sufficient to give a top-gear range of 6–50 mph (10–80 km/h); 40 mph (60–65 km/h) was, however, a comfortable cruising gait, and a gallon of petrol lasted 22 miles (13 lit/100).

Though primarily aimed at the owner driver, it was available in wheelbases up to 132 inches (3.38 m) for formal bodies, electric lighting was standard, and starters a regular option. Total production is not known, but was probably in the region of 500–600 units in four seasons.

Front view of the Delage Type-AK.

1914 Delage Type-AK

Below: three variations on the Isotta Fraschini radiator of 1913/14.

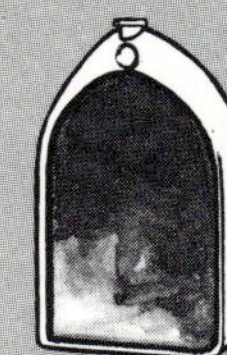

The classic pear shape

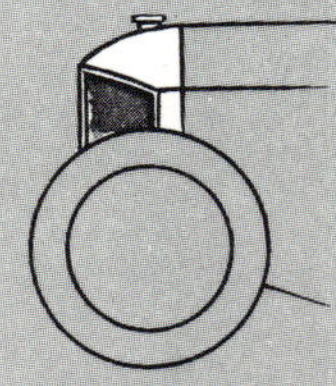

Two types of vee

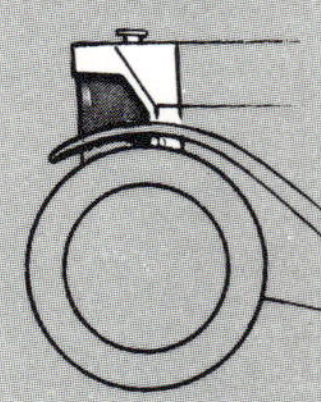

Isotta Fraschini Type-TM

1914, Italy

Not everyone believed in modest capacities and plenty of revs. Others felt that there was no substitute for litres, and even in 1914 there were still some chain-driven giants for enthusiasts who cared nothing for petrol or tyre bills. The 22-litre Blitzen Benz was actually a catalogued model in 1911, though less extreme were the biggest Isotta Fraschinis, the 10.6-litre KM, and the TM illustrated above, of a mere 6.2 litres and 83 bhp. Together they accounted for some 70 units in the 1911–14 period.

Badly hit by the Italian recession of 1907–08, Isotta Fraschini had briefly come under French Lorraine-Dietrich control. By 1909, however, they had bounced back, thanks to the inspired designs of the engineer Cattaneo, and Oreste Fraschini's four-wheel braking system. Isotta's latest giants used four-cylinder, pair-cast engines, with shaft-driven overhead camshafts and two valves per cylinder: crankshafts were pressure-fed. There were four forward speeds, while the brake pedal was linked to drums on the rear wheels and

1914 Nazzaro 20/30hp

transmission: the lever worked on the front wheels only.

For a chassis price of £1,400 in England or $9,000 in the United States, the KM offered 140 bhp and nearly 100 mph (160 km/h), together with a surprising docility. The customer had a choice of three different radiator styles: a pear shape very like that of contemporary Fiats, an aggressive German-style vee, and a gentler vee curiously anticipatory of the post-War 3-litre Bentley. The smaller TM was credited with 70 mph (112 km/h). Just before World War I a shaft-drive edition (Type TC) was offered. After the war, Isotta Fraschini's product, one of the world's first straight eights, became luxurious rather than sporty in character.

Nazzaro 20/30 hp
1914, Italy

Italy's speciality was still the luxury touring car, the medium bracket being typified by the 4½-litre '20/30s' offered by nine firms in 1913/14. Common to all were four cylinders, side valves (usually in an L-head, and cast monobloc), magneto ignition, four-speed gearboxes with right-hand change, and bevel drive. Advertised outputs were in the 30–40 bhp sector, delivered at around 1,500 rpm, and a 3-metre (118-inch) wheelbase was the norm. Further, many of them were look-alikes, with Mercedes-style radiators being phased out in favour of the new pear shape.

Among those who took on the established names (Bianchi, Fiat, Isotta Fraschini, SPA and Züst) was racing driver Felice Nazzaro, long the star of the Fiat works team. His designer was the Swiss, Arnold Zoller, later a pioneer of supercharging, and the Nazzaro was an excellent, if conventional, automobile. Its three-bearing crankshaft was pressure-lubricated, cooling was by pump, and there was a liberal aluminium content (crankcase, gearbox casing, dash, footboards). The clutch was a multiple dry plate, Nazzaro preferred three-quarter-elliptic springs at the rear, and (remarkably) both sets of brakes worked in finned drums on the rear wheels. Detachable steel wheels were standard. Electric lighting was an optional extra in 1914, and the short-chassis Nazzaro Corsa with two-seater body was said to be good for 75 mph (120 km/h).

Alas, Nazzaro was less successful as a manufacturer than as a driver, and he had had enough of building cars by 1916. In any case, the war had halted production after only 230 20/30s had been delivered.

Ohio Electric
1914, United States

Last stronghold of the battery-electric passenger car was the United States, partly because with such a huge motoring population (1,623,739 cars registered in 1914), even a tiny, conservative minority spelt a sizeable overall demand. In the 1909–15 period, the number of electric-car makers never fell below 20, reaching its zenith in 1912, with 27 such firms in the field.

The formula was stereotyped. A series-wound electric motor was mounted under the floor amidships, driving to a differential axle. Body shape was dictated to a large extent by

1914 Ohio Electric

the exigencies of battery stowage, hence the front and rear 'boots'. The base motive power also applied to brakes, gear shift, and even, on some Ohios, to the windows. Also advanced was the curved windscreen, though safety glass was as yet unknown. Maximum performance could be pursued either forwards or backwards, and the electric's lever control enabled it to be conducted from front or rear seat. Though cushion tyres were still listed in 1914, pneumatics were general practice.

Prices were high. At a time when $1,050 (£210) would buy a Buick touring car and $1,575 (£315) a Studebaker Six, both with full electrics, the average electric brougham cost around $3,000 (£600), or more than a closed Cadillac. Open runabouts cost less – Detroit, the leading makers, had one at $2,300 (£460) – but these were seldom encountered. Fuel rationing never hit the United States in World War I, and by the end of the 1920s, only Detroit of the electric car makers were still in business, making the odd vehicle to special order, usually with petrol-car styled bonnet.

Peugeot Bébé
1914, France

Smallest of the new 'big cars in miniature' was Peugeot's Bébé, launched in 1912, and designed by none less than Ettore Bugatti. In production form it made do with two speeds, instead of the five envisaged by its creator.

This was a real miniature on a wheelbase of 71 inches (1.8m), and 103 inches (2.62m) long. The engine, an 856cc T-head four, gave 10bhp and would run up to 2,000rpm. Bugatti-type reversed quarter-elliptic rear suspension was to be expected, but the transmission was ingenious, consisting of two concentric propeller shafts driving bevels, the selection of the ratios being effected by a sliding dog-clutch at the forward end of the propeller shaft. A separate lever was furnished for reverse. A small gearbox was later added in front of the torque tube to transform the vehicle into a three-speeder: it coped with first and reverse. The drip-feed lubricators were tucked away under a streamlined dash and one took one's eye off the road to consult them.

With a top speed of only 35mph (56km/h), a lack of directional stability mattered little. Better news was a tyre consumption estimated at 6,000 miles (nearly 10,000km) a set. The model was in production until 1916, by which time 3,095 had been made. After the war the Bébé was replaced by a more conventional car with L-head engine, differential-less back axle, and a track so narrow that seats had either to be staggered or set in tandem.

Protos 27/65 PS
1914, Germany

Germans, like Italians, were addicted to large cars, the difference being that the former nation sold them at home. Hence no fewer than sixteen models were available in 1914 with capacities in excess of seven litres and advertised outputs between 60 and 105bhp. In this class speeds of 70mph (112km/h) were commonplace, while mechanical specifications embraced everything from T-head hangovers up to the single overhead camshaft of Mercedes's latest 28/95. At 7.2 litres, this last was not much bigger than the heaviest Protos.

That company had been building shaft-drive sixes since 1905. It had raced the type, albeit without success, in the 1907 Kaiserpreis. While the company's entry for the New York-Paris race was a four, sixes went to the House of Hohenzollern: both the Kaiser and the Crown Prince were customers. Protos's designer was the same Ernst Valentin who subsequently worked for Russo-Baltique.

Valentin's engines were of T-head type, cast in pairs, and things changed little after his departure. The pump cooling, dual ignition, and exhaust pressure feed typified this class of car, rear springs were three-quarter-elliptic and the wood wheels wore demountable rims. A heavy vehicle – the chassis alone weighed over 3,000lb (1,400kg) – the Protos was not a spectacular performer. By 1914, familiar improvements were creeping in, notably a more modern L-head power unit. Also present were electric lighting and starting, friction-type shock absorbers, and a power tyre pump. In 14 pre-war years, Protos made approximately 10,000 cars.

1914 Peugeot Bébé

An early Peugeot lion mascot. On later cars (from 1920) the lion stood upright.

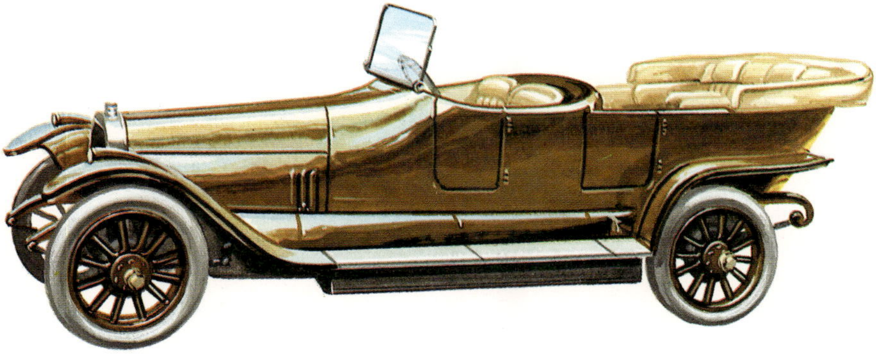

1914 Protos 27/65 PS

1915 Crane-Simplex

Crane-Simplex
1915, United States

Up to 1911, America imported many of her luxury cars, but the rise of the native strain, notably the 'three P's' (Packard, Peerless and Pierce-Arrow), was apparent by 1915, when the state of Massachusetts registered 3,102 Packards and 794 Pierces, but less than 200 Fiats, the most popular foreign breed.

In 1915, Simplex were ready to scrap their chain-drive sports cars. Their successor, designed by Henry M. Crane, cost $6,500 (£1,300) complete. It had six cylinders where the old Simplexes had been content with four, and came on a wheelbase of 143½ inches (3.64m). It was also guaranteed for life while in the original owner's possession; this confidence seems to have been warranted, for trouble-free mileages of 350,000 miles (560,000km) have been recorded.

Even with pressure lubrication, three main bearings sound inadequate on a vast 9-litre engine, but this was conservatively rated, delivering its 110bhp at 2,000rpm. Exhaust pressure feed and pump cooling were fairly general practice, but European influences were apparent in the 12-volt electrics, four-speed gearbox, and transmission footbrake. The spiral bevel back axle was a sign of the times, and of course the car had left-hand steering with central control. With its 'stream line dash' the Crane-Simplex could pass as a 1921 model, and indeed survived uneasily without change into 1924. For a while it formed part of E. S. Hare's luxury-car empire, along with Locomobile and Mercer. One could not, however, emulate General Motors without a Chevrolet in one's locker . . . .

Dodge Four

1915, United States

To launch a new make of cheap automobile two months after the outbreak of a world war, as Dodge did, seems foolhardy. But when that make comes third in the national sales stakes in its first full season, and doubles these sales within two years, it becomes hard to credit.

In the United States, however, military involvement seemed very far away in 1914. Even when President Woodrow Wilson brought the country into the conflict on the Allied side in 1917, civilian production was merely curtailed. And in the intervening years, a technical head start had been matched by formidable export sales. America had cashed in on the car shortage: Britain was taking 4,000 vehicles a month at peak in 1915. There were also places like the Antipodes and South America where Detroit's wares were tailor-made for local conditions, and base price was low enough not to be inflated to ridiculous levels by import duty and freight. Dodges, too, appealed to the Army. The 250 supplied for General Pershing's Mexican expedition in 1916 proved so tough that at least another 9,000 were supplied in the ensuing two years.

The civilian customer, who paid $785 (£157) for his touring or roadster in 1915, got something better than a Ford. Common to both species was a big, slow-turning L-head monobloc four, with detachable head, though Dodge's was bigger (3.5 as against 2.9 litres), and more powerful at 35 bhp. But where Ford stayed with two speeds, Dodge favoured a conventional driveline with a cone clutch and three-speed gearbox. The rear-wheel brakes worked better than Ford's, a starter was standard, and though Dodge's longitudinal suspension was perhaps less tolerant of really impossible going, it could still cope with the rough stuff and give a reasonable highway ride. A sweeter, multiplate clutch was soon adopted, though for many years the make had its own idiosyncrasies – 12-volt electrics instead of the now universal 6-volt, and a back-to-front gear change, with the two higher ratios on the 'wrong' side. (Buick in America and Wolseley in Britain were other long-standing subscribers to this heresy.)

The Dodge Four was destined for a 14-year run, just surviving Chrysler's 1928 takeover. Thereafter it lingered for a further few years in the truck range, and there was even an attempt to revive it as an export-only item in 1932, using Plymouth components. Production passed the 100,000-a-year mark for the first time in 1919, and peaked at 265,000 in 1926. Sedans appeared in 1916 (they were all-steel from 1919) and light commercials took their bow in 1917.

Even in 1915 it was possible to add extras (not always factory-approved) to one's Dodge. This example is certainly laden!

Light van versions of the Dodge Four were made, though bigger trucks were the preserve of the Graham Brothers firm until 1928. This 1926 model has English-built bodywork. It shows few mechanical changes from 1914.

Apperson 8-16

1916, United States

The compact vee-eight engine had been pioneered in France by de Dion-Bouton in 1910, and successfully commercialized five years later by Cadillac in America. By 1916 proprietary V8 engines were bringing the idiom within the reach of lesser firms, though Apperson, of Kokomo, Indiana, made their own, as befitted a pioneer name.

The brothers Edgar and Elmer Apperson were bush mechanics with a railroad background. They had been sponsored by a judge's son, Elwood Haynes, and their prentice experiments of 1894 had grown into a business making two cars a week by 1898. In 1902, however, the Appersons went their own way, progressing via horizontally-opposed, chain-drive twins to big conventional fours. By 1914 they had a six as well, though production was always modest. 1916 would be their best year, with 2,000 of the new eights delivered.

B. J. Hubbard, Apperson's designer, set his two cylinder blocks at 90 degrees, with side valves (of course), fixed heads, and pressure lubrication. The rest of the specification was almost predictable – 6-volt coil ignition, full electrics, a plate clutch, a three-speed gearbox with central change, a spiral bevel back axle, and rear-wheel brakes. Wheelbase was a generous 128 inches (3.25m), and if an 0–40mph (0–64km/h) acceleration time of 20 seconds sounds unimpressive by modern standards, this figure was achieved in top alone, a boon to those who could not double-declutch! At $1,850 (£370), the 8–16 was cheaper than a Cadillac.

Unfortunately, General Motors already offered cheaper V8s (Oakland, Oldsmobile), and Apperson could not compete. They closed their doors in 1926.

1916 Apperson 8-16

1916 Fiat Tipo 70

The Twin-Six mascot used on 1917 Packards.

Fiat Tipo 70

1916, Italy

Here is a true transitional model, bridging the gap between Veteran and Vintage. Though just over 1,000 Tipo 70s were built, and production continued into 1920, few ventured outside their native Italy.

In some respects the Tipo 70 is a car of the early 1920s. The dash is fully streamlined and properly instrumented. Most of the accepted 'Vintage' refinements are present: steel detachable wheels, and 12-volt lighting and starting. Although full-pressure lubrication has yet to come, the three-bearing side-valve engine has a detachable head, and the transmission brake has gone, replaced by two sets of shoes on the rear wheels. Of other familiar features, the magneto still has nearly a decade to go, and so has the simple gravity feed from a tank on the dash. Spiral bevel rear axles will be seen on the true post-war 501, and as yet two litres are seen as the minimum for a family car.

As originally laid down, the 70 had a two-bearing crankshaft and a non-detachable head. It even had the older, Mercedes style of radiator, already dropped from all but the smallest Fiats in 1915. The model's discontinuation immediately after the war was undoubtedly due to Giovanni Agnelli's foresight in recognizing the trend towards higher taxes, and his 1½-litre 501 did everything a 70 did: it cruised quietly at 35 mph (56 km/h). For those who wanted something bigger, there was the parallel 505 of 2.3 litres capacity, with room for seven on a 120-inch (3.048 m) wheelbase.

Packard Twin Six

1916, United States

Greater refinement and flexibility meant more cylinders. Thus the next step forward was a V12. Packard was first, followed by Weidely's proprietary, off-the-peg unit which spawned a flood of short-lived cars of no particular distinction.

The Twin Six, brainchild of J. G. Vincent, was intensively tested, a prototype averaging 15 mpg (18.8 lit/100) over 2,800 road miles. The engine's two blocks were set at an angle of 60 degrees, narrower than a regular (90-degree) V8; there was full-pressure lubrication; and the crankshaft incorporated a Lanchester vibration damper. The carburetter lived in the angle of the blocks, cooling was by twin water pumps, and output was 85 bhp from 7 litres. Packard's traditional transaxle was scrapped in favour of a three-speed unit box: the left-hand, remote-control change was, however, short-lived. All brakes were on the rear wheels, and final drive was by spiral bevel. A power tyre pump was provided as well as full electrics. The car would accelerate to 30 mph (50 km/h) in high gear in 12 seconds. Cylinder heads, fixed in 1916, were made detachable on 1919's Second Series.

A touring car was quite cheap at $3,150 (£630), although post-War inflation and import duty had pushed this up to £2,250 (the equivalent of over $11,000) by the time the model reached Britain in 1920. Over 35,000 Twin Sixes were sold before the model gave way to an even better straight 8 in 1923. In 1921, Warren G. Harding became the first American President to motor to his inauguration – in a 12-cylinder Packard.

Fageol

1917, United States

Traditionally aeronautical influences–overhead camshaft engines and the wider use of light alloys–belong to the Vintage period, while actual aero-engined cars are associated with record work. The high torque and effortless slow running of inline aero motors has, however, a fascination for those who like to travel fast and far, and the application remained viable until designers started to invert these power units in the cause of better streamlining. The snag, of course, was tax: a big-displacement motor such as the 13½-litre Hall-Scott Six in the 1917 Fageol would have been rated at 60 hp in the United States or Britain.

The point was, unfortunately, academic. America's entry into World War I meant that the military wanted Hall-Scott motors in quantity, and the estimate of 20 Fageols built is almost certainly optimistic.

This was a pity, for the car was an engaging monster, and elegant with its wire wheels, sloping radiator, and dinosaur-like opening louvres on the bonnet top. The engine was of overhead-camshaft type with 12 valves, separate cylinders, and ignition by dual magnetos. It developed its impressive 125 bhp at a low 1,300 rpm, and drove the bevel-drive back end via a three-speed gearbox; incredibly, a 1-to-1 axle ratio was a catalogued option. The chassis had side members six inches (15 cm) deep, some reinforcement being secured by mounting engine and gearbox on a bottle-shaped sub-frame. The brakes worked only on the rear wheels, though drums of 16-inch (407 mm) diameter gave a degree of confidence.

Refinement went more than skin-deep, as might be expected at a price of $13,500 (£2,700). Courtesy lamps illuminated the rear number plate, the engine, the running boards, the interior, and even the radiator badge. The badge, as well as the bonnet fasteners, was of carved ivory, while the tool box was lined in plush. Cruising speeds in the high 70s (120–125 km/h) were mentioned, though with high gearing and two-wheel brakes, the car was clearly intended to go rather than to stop.

F. R. Fageol later built trucks and advanced, high-speed motor coaches in Oakland, California.

Overland 4-90

1918, United States

Historically, a 1918 car qualifies as Veteran. Production examples from this year will, however, be American almost without exception. Anything European will be in the form of prototypes for the 1919 model run. In all its essential details, too, the 1918 Overland illustrated below right represents the sort of American automobile that would dominate world export markets over the next few years.

John North Willys had built up an obscure Indiana manufacture from bankruptcy to the Big League. Sales climbed from 4,860 in 1909 to a pre-war peak of 140,111 in 1916. Willys regularly took second place in sales behind Ford. He also built the middle-class Willys-Knight line, and was financially involved in many companies, including Curtiss Aircraft. In addition, he set up component firms like Tillotson (carburetters) and Autolite (electrics) to supply his plants. In 1920 he would make an unsuccessful attempt to manufacture cars in Britain, in association with Crossley of Manchester.

Overland cars had originally used two-speed planetary transmissions, but these had been dropped after 1912. The standard offering now featured a conventional three-speed gearbox, cone clutch, bevel drive, and rear-wheel brakes. From 1916 the separately cast cylinders of the traditional Overland engine had given way to a monobloc casting, while a year later magneto ignition had also gone, in favour of the universal 6-volt coil. Only in the suspension department was any heterodoxy apparent, for at front and rear the cars used pairs of splayed quarter-elliptics, closely akin to Ford's transverse set-up, and nearly as bouncy.

The Overland was rather more expensive than a Ford, and a touring car weighed 2,350 lb (1,067 kg) as against the Ford's 1,500 lb (665 kg). Further, post-war inflation raised the English price from the £225 ($1,125) asked in 1916 to a fearsome £475 ($2,375). The car did, however, have one advantage over Model-T. Though the latter was assembled in Britain, it was offered with left-hand drive only in the early post-war years, right up to the beginning of 1923, whereas Overlands could be had with right-hand steering.

A 1920 version of the Overland Light Four with sedan body and detachable wire wheels.

OR 5885

VINTAGE CARS

Introduction

Motoring for the masses became a reality in the 1920s, even if those masses–outside America–hailed largely from the middle class. Statistics are impressive. America made over four million automobiles in 1928, boosting total registrations by 5 per cent to a record 21,630,000. Ten individual makers produced over 100,000 units apiece.

Nor was this growth confined to the New World. European firms like Citroën, Morris and Renault were good for a cool 50,000 a year; Britain's output of new cars passed the 150,000 mark for the first time in 1926, and even the Great Depression failed to lower annual totals to 1925 levels.

By 1914 standards, cars were cheap. That year, an American paid $975 (just under £200) for an Overland with rear-wheel brakes capable of 45 mph (72 km/h). Electric lights were inclusive, but a starter added $125 (£25) to first cost. By 1929, he was parting with $300 less for the latest in Chevrolets, a six-cylinder where the Overland had been a four, and a four-door sedan instead of an open tourer. Full electrics went without saying, and there were four-wheel brakes. There were also painless, wipe-down-in-an-instant finishes–cellulose and chromium plate. His new model needed less servicing, and what had to be done could be executed on a flat-rate basis at any dealers from Amarillo to Anchorage. Maybe much of the fun had gone out of driving: but then so had the labour and sorrow.

In many ways, the period shows steady evolution rather than outright revolution in car design. Virtues hitherto reserved for rich clients were brought within the reach of the many. Of the main technical elements, only integrally-designed four-wheel brakes had yet to be perfected in 1918, though thanks to World War I, full electrics had yet to cross the Atlantic *en masse*. But mechanical efficiency was on the march, and this becomes apparent when one contemplates European family cars from 1914, 1924 and 1930.

The 1914 norm was a middle-class item. To carry five people at an easy 35–40 mph (60–70 km/h), with 50 mph (80 km/h) on tap where road conditions permitted, one needed some $2\frac{1}{2}$–3 litres of engine giving perhaps 35 bhp at a staid 2,000 rpm, probably less. For this one paid, say, £450. By contrast, typical offerings from the early 1920s were the B-type Citroën, Morris-Cowley and 501 Fiat, all still fours, but good for 18–25 bhp from 1,500 cc. The cost of such a machine in its homeland would not exceed £300, and was likely to be nearer £200. By the end of the 1920s, and despite the greater weight of sedan bodies, even $1\frac{1}{2}$ litres were becoming too big. If true babies in the Austin Seven class were barely four-seaters, the harbinger of things to come was visible in the Peugeot 201, on 1,122 cc perfectly adequate for the needs of a smallish family. (The French, with their infinite ability to cram quarts into pint pots, persuaded it to transport large families as well!)

In the engine department, four cylinders remained in the majority even in the United States to the end of our period–it is salutary to

◀ *Britain's best-selling vintage car, the Morris-Cowley, which helped Morris to a new record of over 54,000 deliveries in 1925. Lights and starter are electric, but front-wheel brakes were not even an option before 1926, and most Cowleys were still open tourers like the one illustrated. Also absent were bumpers, electric wipers and in-built luggage accommodation. Nevertheless, a buyer got 50 mph (80 km/h) and 25 mpg (12 lit/100) for less than £200 ($1,000).*

note that in 1930, all Fords and the cheapest Chrysler and Willys-Overland products were content with such units. Side valves remained essentially the norm; wartime aero-engine influence manifested itself chiefly in the application of light alloys, less so in the spread of sophisticated valve gear, though Wolseley had a 1·3-litre overhead-camshaft light car on the road in 1919, and Singer and Fiat would follow suit in due course. Overhead camshafts were nevertheless found on more expensive machines such as the 1919 6·6-litre Hispano-Suiza and on Lancias from 1922 on. The Knight double-sleeve-valve, a onetime international panacea for noise and vibration, had a limited future. One paid for freedom from the chore of decarbonization with one's own private smokescreen, not to mention high manufacturing costs and the expensive repairs resulting from a seizure. Only Willys in America produced Knights on a mass basis.

Of other under-bonnet features, detachable heads (an aid to servicing) and full-pressure lubrication became general practice. We also encounter the steady abandonment of the magneto (which no layman understood) in favour of coil ignition. The change had already taken place in America during World War I, and by 1930 magnetos were the preserve of more expensive and sporting machinery. European luxury makers like Rolls-Royce favoured dual systems with both magneto and coil.

The safer, rear-mounted fuel tank gained in popularity, though on small and cheap cars gravity feed from a dash tank saw the decade out. Exhaust-pressure systems survived into the mid-1920s on some expensive models, but the nuisance of the initial pump-up by hand killed them. The most popular system of the period was undoubtedly the vacuum type, though both mechanical and electric pumps were gaining ground by 1930.

Transmissions received major attention during the period: not, curiously as yet with actual aids to shifting, even if 1929 Cadillacs featured clashproof synchromesh, and the biggest Armstrong Siddeleys offered the even easier preselector. In Germany, Karl Maybach started by adapting Ford's pedal-controlled two-speed gear to his super-cars before progressing to a far greater complexity. Perhaps here the most significant overall development was the replacement of the cone clutch by the plate type. Not that cones were inherently fierce, but they became so if denied regular maintenance, which the lay motorist could not be expected to furnish.

Instead, designers of the 1920s sought to render shifting superfluous. This principle had

Mass-production comes to Europe. A-type Citroën chassis undergoing final inspection before the mounting of bodies in 1920. Left-hand drive and fully demountable disc wheels are notable features.

Selling the new line. A showroom filled with Henry Ford's brand-new Model-As in 1928, the first major change in 19 years from this maker. Lady customers are much in evidence.

A poster from 1928 promoting the motor-car's acceptance; here it doubles as holiday express and bathing machine.

long been understood in America, where 1918's engines had been big, lazy and capable of doing 90 per cent of their work in top. The multi-cylinder engine had flourished thanks to low manufacturing costs, cheap fuel, the development of crankshaft vibration dampers, and the retention of low engine speeds. It should be remembered that in 1924 the Chrysler's peak revs of 3,200 were considered revolutionary.

To the sixes, V8s and V12s of the 1910–20 period were to be added the straight-eight, which reached its zenith in 1928–29. The snob-appeal of a long bonnet was only part of the story. Even if some of the cheaper horrors were notorious crankshaft-breakers, '0–60 without touching the clutch' was now a reality, while Marmon actually offered a straight-eight for less than $1,000.

Even the term 'light six' took on a new meaning. In 1914 such a machine ran to a hefty 4 litres in Europe, and might well be a $5\frac{1}{2}$-litre in the United States, where 'Big Six' meant over 8 litres, a 135-inch (3·4m) wheelbase, seven seats and a diabolical thirst for tyres. By the end of the war, 3-litre sixes were common in America, and Fiat had a 3·4-litre in production by 1919. From 1926 onward, anything European in the 2/2·5-litre class–Americans seldom built that small–had at least six cylinders, and the end of our period saw the *reductio ad absurdum* with miniatures of 1,500cc or less–low gearing to reconcile weight and flexibility, and of course more of everything to replace, which explains why the wheel had come full circle again by 1935! In the luxury class, of course, painless shifts mattered less: they were the chauffeur's responsibility. Smoothness, of course did, so alongside a whole flood of straight-eights came the twelves of Daimler and Maybach, and Cadillac's splendid V16. Better sound insulation and more sophisticated transmissions would soon render such solutions uneconomic, but they were great while they lasted.

Further aft, the spiral bevel rear axle predominated, accounting for a good 90 per cent of all models. Worm drive had its followers, notably Stutz in America, Lanchester in England, and Peugeot in France, but chains were dead, and found only on the few surviving cyclecars. Underslinging the final drive unit to lower the centre of gravity was a late twenties development found on 1927

Packards and later Rolls-Royce and Lancias, but the hypoid bevel was essentially a late thirties phenomenon. The semi-elliptic spring, likewise, sufficed for most makers, with quarter-elliptics on cheaper cars to keep the cost accountants happy. Independent systems were as yet rare and centred on Germany and Czechoslovakia.

Brakes, by contrast, made immense strides. Outside America in 1914, a transmission-type footbrake and a lever-operated emergency system on the rear wheels had been almost universally accepted. It was still frequently encountered as late as 1923, but four years earlier Hispano-Suiza had led the way with a proper coupled system on all four wheels – and the world's makers followed suit. Inevitably, the mere addition of drums to unmodified front axles riding on narrow-section, high-pressure tyres had interesting consequences, while 1924's newfangled balloon tyre was no solution in itself. By 1927, however, the problems of 'shimmy' had been conquered, and cars without front-wheel brakes were in the minority. As yet, mechanical rod or cable arrangements predominated, despite their stretch-proneness and heavy pedal pressures (hence the servos found on some cheap cars as well as on the expensive heavyweights). Hydraulics were not wholly trustworthy: self-sealing rubber pipe had yet to be perfected.

Electric lighting and starting were a basic feature outside the true utility class even in 1919, but other improvements were on the way. Instrument panels were properly, if unergonomically, stocked, and now that better roads, better tyres and the quick-detachable wheel (universal outside America) had solved the puncture problem, it was time to dispense with cleaning chores. Brass brightwork (always a sartorial nuisance) gave way first to nickel and then to maintenance-free chromium plate. As for paint-and-varnish, with its costly and frequent demands for renewal, this had no place on a hack condemned to 12,000 annual miles of all-weather usage. Hence DuPont's Duco cellulose, first seen on 1924's Oaklands and almost universal in 1930.

A curious development of the period was the leather-covered flexible fabric body, aimed more at cutting down weight and eliminating drumming. Fashionable in Europe between 1925 and 1930, it was even easier to clean, but its self-disintegrating tendencies killed it. So did its matt finish in an era when women clients were being wooed with brighter colours.

Bodies, now largely the chassis maker's responsibility, progressed. The new painless-motoring theme called for closed coachwork, now economically viable thanks to growing demand and more efficient engines to take the extra weight. The remaining major problem – a price increment of nearly 70 per cent – was finally overcome by Hudson with their cheap Essex Coach of 1921, and by 1929 90 per cent of the world's new cars were sedans and coupés rather than roadsters and tourers. This led to the curious situation in America where the more basic closed styles actually cost less than open types. Rattles and squeaks were gradually banished by the elimination of wood from structures: Citroën had an all-steel sedan in production by 1925, and the American pioneers of this system, Budd of Philadelphia, ensured its spread by opening associate factories in Oxford and Berlin.

A sedan body might be cheap, and not impossibly heavy. It might also stand up to the pounding of bad roads (though significantly in countries with suitable climates and poor highways, notably Australia, the tourer remained popular well into the 1930s). Its all-weather potential might be excellent even before the advent of heaters, screenwashers or efficient screenwipers. But it lacked one thing: looks. Hence the rise of the stylist.

Not that he was regarded, even in 1930, as an integral part of the creation of an automobile. But increasingly manufacturers sought to integrate design, and not to regard coachwork as a mere appendage to the mechanical elements. In this respect, the pioneering Lanchester brothers of the early 1900s had their Vintage counterpart in Gabriel Voisin, who possessed decided (and eccentric) ideas on bodies. Alongside such individualists, however, was Harley Earl, of General Motors, creator of the 1927 La Salle. Following in his footsteps came Al Leamy with the long, low look of the 1929 front-wheel drive Cord. In Britain, a youthful William Lyons was transforming the homely Austin Seven into his curvaceous Swallow with two-tone 'strawberries-and-cream' paintwork. The growing ranks of lady motorists need no longer feel aesthetically ashamed of what they parked outside the tennis club.

Alas, the eccentrics were on the way out. Nobody strayed far from the *système Panhard*, with its frontal engine driving the rear wheels. None of the front-wheel drive creations of the period – Britain's Alvis, France's Tracta, America's Cord and Ruxton – made a major impact, and rear-engined machinery was equally rare, despite the success of the 1925 Hanomag Kommissbrot in Germany. In

America, indeed, the norm was strict. A typical family model of 1928 would be a side-valve six with coil ignition, vacuum feed, and three-speed gearbox. The clutch would be a dry-plate, and the orthodox chassis frame would be hung on four semi-elliptic springs. Drive would be transmitted to a spiral bevel back end, and the brakes (partly or wholly of contracting type) would work on all four wheels. Wheelbase variations were inevitable, but regardless of the make or price, the track would be a uniform 56 inches (1·42 m).

And what America thinks today, Europe thinks tomorrow. Sports cars might retain their individuality, but the other eccentricities were going overboard. The cyclecar was dead by 1925, despite French attempts to give it a legal definition based on a maximum permitted weight of 350 kilograms. Its barbarities could not compete against the flood of 5CV Citroëns, their Opel cousins, Austin Sevens, and 509 Fiats. Tax loopholes, especially in Britain, would give the three-wheeler a further lease of life, but the well-loved Morgan was essentially a sociable two-seater for sporting motor-cyclists rather than sub-utility transportation.

As for alternative power, it faded away. Steam and electric vehicles are included in this book to show the state of the art such as it was, but neither system had any currency outside America. And even there, it would be surprising if the decade's total production – most of it Stanleys delivered between 1919 and 1926 – exceeded 3,000 units. Of the steamers, Abner Doble's superb Model-E triumphed over almost every past weakness of the system, but its price of around £2,500 limited its impact to the favoured few – and even they did not want it.

The electric brougham had even less appeal. Conservative customers were well content with 1910's china-cupboard styling, and with the wholesale acceptance of motoring, there were few who wanted a vehicle with a top speed of 30 mph (50 km/h) and a maximum range between charges of 75 miles (120 km) – especially since one-fifth of the money would buy a dependable gasoline runabout capable of long runs if required.

A motor-car for everyone, though one doubts if in 1922 a working-class family could have afforded this £165 Austin. Conceived as minimal transportation for two adults and two children, it replaced the motor-cycle combination in better-off households.

For the wealthy, there was elegance – at a price. Few later stylists have surpassed this 1930 Phantom II Rolls-Royce sedanca de ville by Barker. But £3,000 in those days would be the equivalent of at least £60,000 today.

Angus-Sanderson 14 hp
1919, Great Britain

The Angus-Sanderson was an early British dream of mass-production. The concept was admirable and, in some ways, an anticipation of future techniques, in that essential components were to be bought-out from specialists – engines by Tylor, and gearboxes by Wrigley. The parent firm, as coachbuilders, handled bodies themselves. The promised price of under £400 for a family five-seater was inviting.

The car was conventional: a side-valve 2·3-litre four with three-speed gearbox and bevel drive. Rear springing was cantilever, while modern thinking was reflected in the central gearchange, full electrics, and absence of a transmission brake. As yet the British taxation system had not been revised to penalize a vehicle rated at 15 hp.

Unfortunately, trouble soon loomed. Post-war industrial unrest was bad enough, but the assembly plant's location in County Durham was too far away from the industry's mainstream. The weekly target of 50 cars was never achieved, hence the price rose steadily, from £450 in 1919 to a less realistic £575 before customers laid hands on a single Angus-Sanderson. True, 3,000 had been made by 1921, but the company was bankrupt.

Angus-Sanderson struggled on into 1927 with a move to Hendon (London), two re-organizations and a belated effort to produce a small car which never passed the prototype stage. Latter-day production was, however, largely a case of using up the parts stockpiled in 1919.

Buick H
1919, United States

American cars had acquired left-hand drive and full electrics by 1914; two years later dashes had been streamlined into bonnets. Production was achieving formidable levels, with only minor disruption from World War I. Buick's 1919 deliveries of 119,310 units were beaten only by Ford and Chevrolet, an impressive performance for a middle-class automobile selling in its homeland for $1,595 (about £320). But then the make was respected as 'The Doctor's Friend' as far afield as Australia and South Africa.

American engineering was predictable. Although cone clutches and semi-pressure lubrication were old-fashioned and European motorists might have preferred four forward speeds, the customer got full electrics and foolproof coil ignition. All brakes were on the rear wheels, and whereas in Europe a 4-litre tourer weighing $1\frac{1}{2}$ tons would have made do with four-cylinders, its American counterpart was a six with (exceptionally in America) overhead valves. The cylinder head was, however, non-detachable and would stay that way till 1924. The principal novelty of 1919 was the illuminated instrument board.

Mass-production permitted a choice of body, if not colour. The H-series Buick came as a roadster, touring, coupé or sedan, though closed models were not as yet exported, and cost a cool 25 per cent more than open types. Thus the latter outnumbered the former by 20-to-1. Not everyone, of course, liked the American idiom (styling as a science did not exist), so the British importers offered their own custom bodies, which included some quite elegant cabriolets.

1919 Angus-Sanderson 14 hp.

◀*Exposed valve gear characterized pre-1924 Buick engines. This one dates from 1916, and is a four-cylinder.*

Citroën A
1919, France

Before World War I, few European factories had potentials of more than 5,000 cars a year and moving assembly lines were unknown. André Citroën changed all this with his Model-A: though a new manufacturer, he had already made his fortune with herring-bone bevel gears.

The car which went on sale in the summer of 1919 was the brainchild of Jules Salomon, designer of the little single-cylinder Le Zèbre. Citroën's A was, however, a bigger four for four people on a long $111\frac{1}{2}$-inch (2·835 m) wheelbase, with 1·3-litre side-valve engine, detachable head, three-speed unit gearbox, central change (convenient for left or right-hand steering), and spiral bevel back axle. The footbrake worked on the transmission, and money was saved by the use of quarter-elliptic springs and gravity feed. An engine turning at only 2,100 rpm did not need a fan, but electrics and a spare wheel were inclusive for the £500 initially asked in Britain. No wonder Citroën were shipping 30 cars a day across the Channel by 1920. Economy was exemplary – 38 mpg (7·5 lit/100) on the open road and 30 (9·5 lit/100) in town, though the splash lubrication called for a pint of oil every 130 miles (1 litre every 470 km). By the end of 1921 the company had sold over 28,000 cars, all Model-As.

Citroën's badge represents the double herring-bone gears that made his name.

Hispano-Suiza H6

1919, France

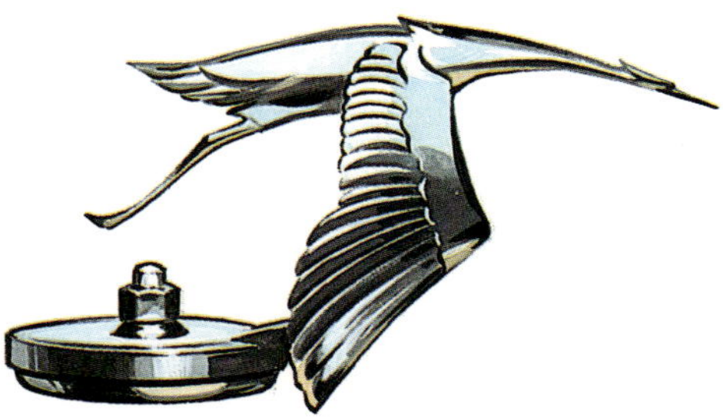

Hispano-Suiza's Flying Stork mascot.

The large Hispano-Suiza front brake drum.

If the Silver Ghost Rolls-Royce had been the model luxury tourer in the 1907–14 period, Marc Birkigt's six-cylinder Hispano-Suizas would assume its mantle as the Vintage yardstick of excellence. True, some of the Ghost's silence had been lost–connoisseurs spoke of 'marine engine' noises from under the bonnets of the new Franco-Spanish machine–but output had been tripled, and even a limousine-bodied H6 was faster than a Ghost wearing light tourer coachwork.

During World War I, over 30,000 of the Swiss designer's V8 aeromotors had been supplied to the Allied air forces: the car had been under development alongside these since 1915. Aeronautical influence was detectable in the light-alloy cylinder block and pistons, in the tubular steel connecting-rods, in the full-pressure lubrication, and in the shaft-driven overhead camshaft. The seven-bearing crankshaft was machined from a solid billet of steel; further, it was innocent of those tooth-shaking 'periods' that had bedevilled many a pre-war six. American influence was also present: Birkigt preferred coils to magnetos, though he used a duplicated system with 12 sparking plugs. Fuel was fed by vacuum from a rear tank to the dual-choke carburetter. In Birkigt's view, three forward speeds were sufficient to transmit the 6·6-litre engine's 135 bhp.

Beautifully constructed on aero-motor lines, the Hispano-Suiza engine is stove-enamelled black and features dual coil ignition.

Even more sophisticated was the chassis. Admittedly it rode on orthodox semi-elliptic springs, and the first H6s lacked even friction-type dampers, but Birkigt had been one of the first designers to utilize unit construction of engine and gearbox as frame reinforcement, and his latest braking arrangements offered a degree of retardation unheard of in 1919. Four-wheel brakes were, of course, known, but the Hispano's were not only of coupled type (the pedal was linked to all four wheels), but were also energized by a servo motor driven off the gearbox. In addition, the light-alloy drums were finned for better cooling. Early Hispano servos sometimes lost effect below about 15 mph (25 km/h): nevertheless Rolls-Royce would adopt the system (and pay royalties for it) from 1923 onward.

Other modern features were in evidence. Wheels were of quick-detachable, centre-lock wire type, and every H6 had full instrumentation, including a rev counter (peak power was developed at 3,500 rpm). A further refinement was a power tyre pump taking its drive from the gearbox.

The car went into production at Hispano-Suiza's two factories in Barcelona and Paris, Spanish versions being identifiable by their cast-iron blocks. One of the first customers was, of course, Birkigt's old patron, King Alfonso XIII of Spain. For the £3,000-odd he and others paid, they got a car capable of outrunning all but the fastest of 1914's sports models – 80–85 mph (130/140 km/h) allied to an 0–60 mph (0–100 km/h) acceleration time of half a minute, and the ability to potter along at a walking pace in top. Roadholding was excellent, which explains how the millionaire André Dubonnet was able to average 41 mph (66 km/h) over the 540 miles (864 km) from Paris to Nice in 1921. The H6 was also most durable, mileages of 250,000 (400,000 km) being commonplace between major overhauls.

Above all, the car had elegance. Its radiator was crowned by the flying stork emblem worn by the Hispano-powered aircraft of Georges Guynemer's wartime squadron, and it attracted some of the best-looking custom coachwork of the 1920s. The model was destined for a 15-year run, during which over 2,600 were delivered. A further 50 were made under licence in Czechoslovakia by Skoda; the first one, appositely, went to President Thomas Masaryk. By 1924, enthusiasts could have the short-chassis 8-litre Boulogne edition, capable of 100 mph (160 km/h) on 144 bhp.

And even if the Hispano itself was reserved for the favoured few – price never fell far below the £2,000 mark – its influence turned up in unlikely places. America's first factory-styled automobile, the 1927 La Salle (see page 58) was Hispano-inspired, while the genesis of the overhead-camshaft MG family can be traced back to the 10·5 hp Wolseley of 1919, itself a spin-off of the Birmingham concern's war work – licence-production of the V8 Hispano aero engine.

The Sunbeam's ancestor, with which Victor Rigal won the 1912 Coupe de l'Auto race. Speeds of 85–90 mph (135–145 km/h) were extracted from its simple side-valve engine.

Sunbeam 16hp
1919, Great Britain

If in their different ways Hispano-Suiza and Citroën were creating a new idiom in cars, other more conservative firms were making do in 1919 with warmed-over 1914 machinery. The well-loved 16hp Sunbeam differed only from its pre-war counterpart in its spiral bevel rear end, half instead of three-quarter elliptic rear springs, and electric starter. The 1914 cars already featured electric lights and 'stream line' bonnets.

Yet this stolid tourer, with its long-stroke 3-litre four-cylinder engine giving a sedate 35 bhp, had an excellent pedigree. It had been around since 1911, while competition versions had shown their mettle with victory in the 1912 *Coupe de l'Auto* light car race, thanks to engines tuned to give 74 bhp and a resultant maximum of 90 mph (145 km/h). The regular model had served as a staff car in the late war; owing to Sunbeam's aero-engine commitments, War Office production had been entrusted to Rover.

Engineering was traditional – magneto ignition, a non-detachable head, a four-speed separate gearbox with right-hand change and central accelerator, and a leather cone clutch. Standard brightwork was in brass, but sadly inflation had boosted the price of a tourer from its pre-war £442 to a swingeing £1,225 by the end of 1919.

For a heavy car, the Sunbeam was quite frugal: 20–22 mpg (13–14 lit/100), while tyres were said to last 7,000 miles (over 10,000 km). By 1922 the 16 had acquired overhead valves; four-wheel brakes came a year later, and for the 1924 season the big four gave way to a six.

Ansaldo 4C
1920, Italy

After the 1918 Armistice, many ordnance firms found themselves with nothing to do. In such a case were Ansaldo, Italy's main ordnance company, who sought to challenge Fiat's domination with their overhead-camshaft 4A, the work of Guido Soria.

His car looked uncommonly like a Chevrolet, with its simple tourer body and wood wheels, though these latter were fully demountable. Also American in concept was the three-speed gearbox with its central change, while the gravity feed, spiral bevel back axle and semi-elliptic springs were conventional enough. The footbrake worked on the rear wheels, but more interesting was the engine, a neat little monobloc overhead-camshaft four with detachable head, giving 35 bhp from 1·7 litres. Top speed, at 55 mph (88 km/h) was only about 7 mph (11 km/h) faster than Fiat's side-valve 501, but a later touring Ansaldo would show its toughness by averaging 45 mph (72 km/h) over 10,000 miles (16,000 km).

Alas, the home market was weak, and Fiat had the lion's share of exports. Though Ansaldo did well in some countries, notably New Zealand, annual production stayed below 1,000 units. Not even an improved 2-litre capable of 70 mph (112 km/h) could save the day. Soria tried an overhead-camshaft six and a $3\frac{1}{2}$-litre straight-eight, but after his resignation in 1927 Ansaldo's automobile activities faded quietly away.

Armstrong Siddeley 30

1920, Great Britain

In 1919 J. D. Siddeley merged his Siddeley-Deasy company with Armstrong Whitworth's car division, to produce 'Cars of Aircraft Quality' for 40 years.

His prototype was the 'all aluminium' Marmon 34 from America, and Marmon influences were detectable in the six-cylinder overhead-valve engine, three-bearing crankshaft, three-speed gearbox with central control, gravity feed, and cantilever rear suspension. The chassis, of 140-inch (3·55 m) wheelbase, incorporated the running boards, but for all its liberal use of aluminium the big Siddeley, unlike the Marmon, was no great performer on 60 bhp from 5 litres. Further, its aggressive vee-radiator crowned by a Sphinx mascot made it an ugly creature contrasting sharply with the Marmon's elegance.

Siddeley hoped to make 5,000 30s a year, hardly a viable proposition for a £1,000 car in those hard times. What he was quick to achieve was royal patronage: the Duke of York (later King George VI) took delivery of his first Armstrong Siddeley in the summer of 1920, adding a second one in 1921. By 1923 front-wheel brakes were a catalogued option; monobloc instead of pair-cast cylinders came on 1925's Mk II; and four years later the 30 became the first car to be offered with the Wilson preselective transmission as standard equipment. By this time the company's range included smaller fours and sixes for the owner-driver.

1920 Ansaldo 4C

◀ *Armstrong Siddeley's Sphinx mascot, sitting up on early cars.*

1920 Armstrong Siddeley 30

Cole Aero 8

1920, United States

Cadillac's 1915 V8 had many imitators, thanks to the proprietary-engine industry: for smaller American makers, Northway and Herschell-Spillman offered instant, off-the-peg units. General Motors's Oakland Division had, indeed, made brief use of the same Northway eight that had powered every Indianapolis-built Cole from 1916 to the end nine years later.

Coles were closer in size and price to Cadillacs than to Oaklands. They were big cars on a 127-inch (3·225m) wheelbase, good for 75mph (120km/h) with a thirst of 12–14 mpg (20–23lit/100). Ignition was by coil, the clutch was a cone, and the rest was the American norm: three-speed unit gearbox, expanding and contracting brakes on the rear wheels only, and semi-elliptic springs with friction dampers. Equipment included a power tyre pump, while closed bodies were afflicted with unattractive names such as 'Tourosine'.

At peak in 1919 Cole sold 5,000 cars, but such small firms could not remain competitive. Nor had they the organization to support serious export drives, though Coles enjoyed a brief currency in Britain in 1920–21, handled (oddly) by Hammersmith coachbuilder William Cole. The last Aero-Eights were among the first cars to fit balloon tyres as standard.

The Cole Aero 8 aptly had a propeller motif with its temperature gauge.

1920 Cole Aero 8

SB

1920, Germany

The cyclecar enjoyed a brief revival during the stringent economic climate of 1919–21. The German SB (Slaby-Beringer) was an oddball even by the barbarous standards of its class: it was a battery-electric.

Likened by one writer to 'a beer crate on pram wheels', it was of all-wood unitary construction: designer Rudolf Slaby had worked on aircraft during the war. The box-like miniature was a single-seater, 82 inches (2·08m) long and $41\frac{1}{2}$inches (1·05m) wide. The underfloor-mounted motor transmitted its power by chain to the left rear wheel: there was no differential. The 19th-century appearance (an SB actually found its way into a Brighton Run for Veteran cars before its provenance was discovered!) was heightened by the fixed wire wheels, tiller steering, and spoon brakes working, Benz-fashion, on the rear tyres. Fortunately there was also a transmission brake, though unlike other electrics, the SB depended on oil lamps for illumination, and even these were extra!

There must, however, have been some market for such sub-utility transportation, for Gamages' store acquired the British agency, and some SBs were sold in the Far East. By 1922, the car had grown into a tandem two-seater using a 3hp two-stroke DKW motor-cycle engine, while at least one SB acquired a dummy nose-radiator to give it a more automobile-like appearance.

▼ *Good workmanship, and plenty of aluminium on the Secqueville-Hoyau's firewall. Right-hand steering and controls still predominated in France.*

Secqueville-Hoyau Type-A

1920, France

Miniature luxury cars are usually associated with Britain. The Secqueville-Hoyau, however, came from a French factory with an interest in Bugatti aero engines, a connection which explains why contemporary reports called it (erroneously) an Ettore Bugatti design. The 'baby Rolls' label was a truer bill, since radiator and bonnet were shamelessly cribbed from the great British make.

The car was a conventional little three-bearing, side-valve four giving 18 bhp from 1·2 litres. Likewise to be expected was the magneto ignition, but, in this class, four forward speeds, full-pressure lubrication, centre-lock wire wheels, and vacuum feed from a rear tank were genuine big-car refinements. Springs were semi-elliptic, whereas Citroën were content with quarter-elliptics. All brakes worked on the rear wheels, and detail finish was first-class, down to an engine-turned dash. Bodies offered included a pretty little four-seater saloon and a chauffeur-driven *coupé de ville*, this wide range rendered viable by a choice of three wheelbase lengths. Full electrics were, of course, standard.

Unfortunately, all this cost three times the price of a Type-A Citroën, and though the make was still quoted in 1923, production was probably less than 600 units. At the end, cars were being offered with overhead-valve engines and front-wheel brakes: on paper there was even a 1·8-litre six, though it it is doubtful if any such cars reached the public.

1920 SB

Marmons appealed to the wealthier motorist on both sides of the Atlantic; the royal family of Norway had at least two. In the 1920s, American Presidents generally preferred Pierce-Arrows, but here is Woodrow Wilson taking part in a ceremonial parade in California just after World War I. The patriotic decorations make it hard to spot the Marmon 34 underneath.

Marmon 34

1921, United States

Prototype for the Armstrong Siddeley 30 (page 19), the Marmon 34 had been on the market since 1916. It was not a cheap car: price was $4,250, far above the $3,590 asked for a V8 Cadillac, or even the $3,950 of Mercer's sporting L-Head Four. There were, of course, marked similarities with the Siddeley, notably the six-cylinder overhead-valve bi-block engine with its three-bearing crankshaft, though by this time the magneto had given way to the usual American 6-volt coil ignition. Marmon preferred double transverse springs to the Armstrong Siddeley's longitudinal semi-elliptics at the rear, and the car's 5·5-litre engine gave 74 bhp compared to the British machine's 60 bhp from 5 litres. Both cars featured robust Z-section frames.

On the original 34s the aluminium content had been impressive–for block, crankcase, valve gear, water pump, engine mountings, differential casing, radiator shell, bonnet, and body panels, though body framing was in ash. Mechanical troubles, however, led to a redesign in 1920 with a cast-iron block. None the less, the 34 was still a brisk performer, capable of 75–80 mph (120–130 km/h); a stock tourer did a standing lap of Indianapolis Speedway at 63·2 mph (101·1 km/h).

The Marmon's appearance was handsome, with a pearshaped radiator rather in the Fiat idiom, and most Marmons wore wire detachable wheels instead of the usual American fixed wood equipment with demountable rims. Unusually for a luxury car (but again like the Siddeley), the 34 carried its fuel in a 20-gallon (100-litre) tank on the dash. Rear tanks came on later models, along with balloon tyres and four-wheel brakes, but so expensive a car could not sell in large numbers, and Marmon could not keep going on a mere 3,000 units a year. In 1927 there was a swing in the direction of cheaper straight-eights, which helped the Indianapolis factory see the decade out.

Milburn
1921, United States

By 1921 battery-electrics were on their way out. Only in the United States did firms like Anderson (Detroit), Rauch & Lang and Milburn struggle on. As internal-combustion engines grew more refined, their hopes faded. Not only were there the known limitations of speed and range: the clientele was elderly and conservative, and on an electric there was nothing to wear out.

Though some later electrics masqueraded as petrol cars, with dummy bonnets – Milburn themselves offered such devices – the old 'china cupboard' shape predominated, with lever steering, and short decks front and rear which housed the batteries. On Milburns these latter were mounted on rails so that they slid out for recharging. The motor lived amidships underfloor, transmitting its power to a worm-drive back axle. Long cantilever rear springs gave a good ride.

Controls were simple. The four forward speeds and auxiliary electric brake were lever-actuated, with pedals for both mechanical brakes. One pedal incorporated a ratchet for parking, the other working the release mechanism. A third pedal engaged reverse, giving four speeds in either direction. Milburn claimed 30 mph (50 km/h), a range of 80 miles (128 km) and low-speed acceleration comparable to a conventional 2½-litre car.

For all its compact dimensions – length was 138 inches (3·5 m) – the Milburn was no cheap runabout. In England it cost as much as a big Sunbeam or Vauxhall, and the $2,685 asked on the home market represented the price of two Dodges. A factory fire in 1922 administered the *coup de grâce*.

1921 Milburn

Protos C
1921, Germany

While new ranges were being announced elsewhere, Germany lagged behind. Barred by the vindictive Allies from many export markets, and bedevilled by galloping domestic inflation, she made do with warmed-over 1914 designs. These were little changed apart from their full electrics and ugly, aggressive vee-radiators, the hallmark of a 'sports' model in pre-war days.

The Protos typified such thinking. Its fixed-head, side-valve four-cylinder engine gave only 30 bhp from 2·6 litres, the four-speed gearbox was separately-mounted, and the footbrake worked on the transmission. Wheels were wood with demountable rims: modern thinking was confined to the full-pressure lubrication and vacuum feed. It was a big and heavy (3,300 lb/1,520 kg) machine on a 126-inch (3·2 m) wheelbase.

Sales were surprisingly good in view of the economic situation, running as high as 150 a month. Protos's parent firm, Siemens, were, however, disenchanted with motor-cars, and sold Protos to the rival AEG combine. They, in their turn, merged the firm with Presto and NAG, only the last-mentioned make continuing after 1927.

1921 Protos C

Rover 8

1921, Great Britain

Rover's long-standing pre-eminence in the upper echelons of the British family-car market makes one tend to forget that the firm's name was made with inexpensive lightweights, from the 6- and 8-hp singles of 1904–12 to the less attractive worm-drive 10/25 line which lingered on into 1933. The ancestor of this latter was the 8, a halfway stage between the cyclecar and the truly modern babies such as the Peugeot Quadrilette and Austin's Seven (pages 30–1). Rover's challenger was announced at the 1919 London show, this Mark Wild design (illustrated below) being listed for six years, to the tune of some 17,000 units produced. The car was simple. It was also cheap, progressive reductions halving 1921's list price (£300) by 1924. It rewarded its makers amply for its then-fearsome tooling bill of £400,000.

Chassis-wise, no cyclecar influences were to be seen. The steel frame might be primitive and ride on quarter-elliptic springs, but the drive line was of proper car type–a single-plate clutch, a three-speed box with central ball change, and a worm back axle. Both sets of brakes worked on the rear wheels, while the rack-and-pinion steering anticipated today's practice.

Under the bonnet, things were somewhat cruder. Power came from a short-stroke side-valve 1-litre flat-twin engine with splash lubrication and air cooling, which kept weight down and noise up, the latter accentuated by the car's disc wheels. In an era when starters were becoming mandatory, the Rover had no provision for one before 1922, though by this time regular equipment included speedometer, clock, and side curtains. A dynamo driven off the propeller shaft took care of the three-lamp lighting set.

Apart from cylinder heads projecting through the bonnet sides–contrary to rumour these did *not* glow cherry-red when the engine was hot–appearance was conventional, with a dummy radiator. As everyday transport, it had much to commend it. Top speed was a leisurely 38 mph (61 km/h) in standard form, or over 50 (80 km/h) with Frazer Nash's proprietary overhead-valve conversion. An owner-survey taken in 1923 indicated average fuel consumptions of 43 mpg (6·5 lit/100), while engines consumed a gallon of oil every 740 miles (5 litres every 1,185 km).

In 1921 the two-seater was still the staple 8, but an occasional four-seater and a pretty little coupé (a starter was inclusive on this one) came in 1923, and a year later the range was extended to embrace open and closed four-seaters on a longer chassis, the latter being one of Britain's first catalogued Weymann fabric saloons. To cope with additional weight, capacity went up to 1,130 cc and output from 13 to 16·5 bhp. Also available was a light van for quarter-ton payloads.

►*A publicity picture of the Rover 8 chassis. Inclining the engine downwards put the starting handle at the best height for cranking; this was desirable because there was no starter, and the car was a brute to start from cold. There were also only three nuts to undo when changing a wheel.*

▼ *Rover's regular coupé bodies were of fixed-head type, and this neat little cabriolet was probably a special order. The varnished wood window-framing was a refinement. Night driving must have been a headache with such tiny, cowl-mounted lamps, the sole frontal illumination.*

▼ *On a very cheap car one did not expect a fully-stocked dashboard: the Rover's was notably bare. The central gear lever was cranked to bring it easily to hand, and interior furnishings were of the simplest. The bulge in the bonnet side accommodates one cylinder of the flat-twin engine, as well as admitting cooling air.*

By this time the car had a loyal following: an owners' club was formed and in 1924, the peak year, some 5,000 found buyers. It was, however, always tricky to start from cold, and starters remained an extra to the end. Even after the addition of an oil pump it was also a notorious crankshaft-breaker, which explains the model's high mortality rate. In the late 1920s one well-known spare part specialist built his father a garage – on a foundation of 600 disc wheels off discarded Rovers! The end came in 1925, when the 8 gave way to a less interesting 1,074cc water-cooled four-cylinder nine.

Studebaker Light Six

1921, United States

Studebaker had been building wagons since 1852, hence the wheel badge.

By the early 1920s, six-cylinder engines had spread to the lower-middle-class sector of the American market. Further, 'Light Sixes' were just that, and not – as they had been in 1916 – hefty $4\frac{1}{2}$-litre machines which were merely less unwieldy than their companion 'Big Sixes'. In 1921, Studebaker had not only abandoned fours for good, but reduced their cheapest model to a manageable 3·4-litre capacity, 2,400 lb (1,090 kg) of weight, and a compact 112 inches (2·845 m) of wheelbase. Even in a slump they could sell the finished product at home for less than $1,500 (£300), which explains why the company stayed in America's Top Ten, and took fourth place in 1921's national sales stakes.

Engineering was copybook American. The side-valve power unit was vacuum-fed and splash-lubricated, with pump cooling and 6-volt coil ignition. The cylinder head was, of course, detachable, and drive was taken by a single-plate clutch and three-speed gearbox (still, surprisingly, separate from its engine) to a spiral bevel rear end. Also old-fashioned by local standards was the use of a separate sub-frame for motor and gearbox. Contracting-and-expanding brakes worked on the rear wheels; detachable wire wheels were a seldom-seen extra. Like Ford, Studebaker offered only black to home-market customers, though British buyers got their Light Sixes in blue or fawn, and could even specify London-made landaulette coachwork. For those who felt that 45 bhp and 50 mph (80 km/h) were inadequate, the company offered bigger cars. At the top of the range was a 5·8-litre 'heavy' on a 126-inch (3·2 m) wheelbase.

A Temperino at the start of the 1921 Brooklands 200-Mile Race; behind is one of the victorious 1,100 cc Salmsons. Driving on this occasion was the English importer J. S. Wood, but few Temperinos were sold anywhere; the day of the cyclecar was almost over. Even dummy radiators still aped Fiat's classic 1913 pear shape.

1921 Temperino

Temperino
1921, Italy

As yet, Italy concentrated on relatively big cars for export; her smallest model to sell in numbers in the 1920s was Fiat's 1-litre 509 (pages 54–5). Cyclecars had no future: there were no domestic marginal motorists to buy them, while good foreign customers (Britain, France) made their own. Thus it is remarkable that the Torinese Temperino lasted six seasons, dying only from the same bank collapse that brought down SPA (page 34).

Italian touring-car styling is often imitative, and by 1919 many makers favoured the pear-shaped radiator initiated by Fiat in 1911. On Temperinos, however, this was a dummy; in the best cyclecar traditions the firm used an aircooled vee-twin unit, its circulation assisted by a belt-driven wooden fan. This engine was set transversely, driving via a multi-plate clutch to a three-speed transaxle incorporating a differential.

There were some crudities. Gear and brake levers lived out of doors in the interests of elbow-room, rear springs were quarter-elliptic, and what looked like a conventional starting handle was in fact a motor-cycle-type kick starter. Wheels were very small for the period, and, with an eye on the French cyclecar laws, weight was kept down to 350 kg (770 lb). This meant no electrics: acetylene lamps sufficed. Surprisingly, plans were laid to make Temperinos in Britain; less surprisingly, these plans came to naught.

Audi 14/50 PS
1922, Germany

When August Horch latinized his name to Audi and set up down the street in Zwickau in opposition to his old firm, the venture prospered initially. In the 1920s, however, Audi suffered from a range which, though modern by German standards, was far too expensive to make. A total of 750 Ks at most were produced in a three-year run, so it is no wonder that the directors were negotiating for a reconciliation with the Horchwerke. This would not come about until the formation of the Auto Union group in 1932.

Helmut Lange's first post-war design was interesting, if only as the first German car to go on sale with left-hand steering. Its 3·6-litre four-cylinder pushrod engine was pressure-lubricated, and featured a light-alloy block and pistons. The axle casing was also of aluminium, cooling was by thermo-siphon, and the carburetter was fed by an Autovac. The gearshift was directly mounted on the box in the centre, and Audis came complete with centre-lock wire wheels, power tyre pumps, and tilting steering wheels, though not with front wheel brakes: these (complete with hydraulics and a servo) were reserved for the even costlier M-type six of 1925. Model-K looked sporting enough with its characteristic vee-radiator, but even a bare chassis weighed well over 3,000 lb (1,400 kg) and performance was unspectacular.

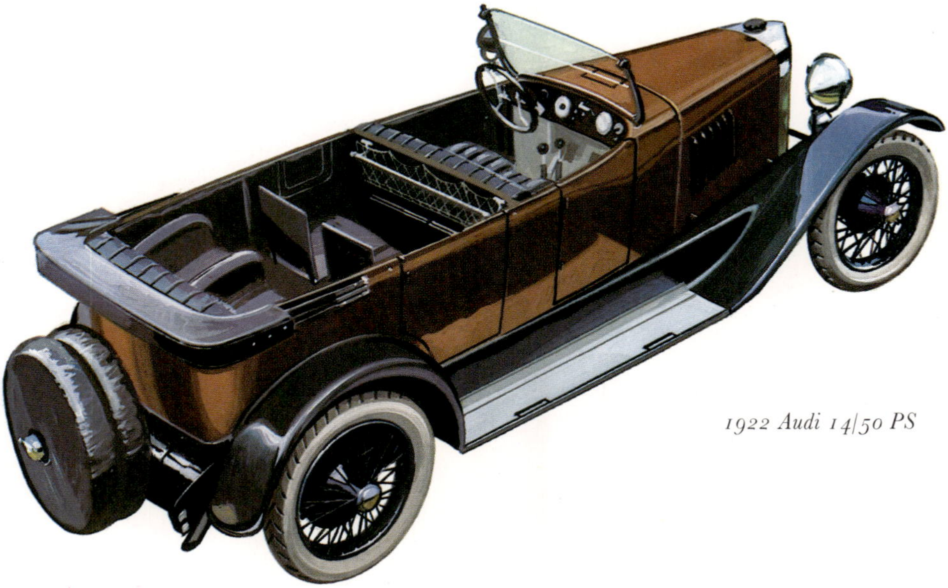

1922 Audi 14/50 PS

Elizalde T48

1922, Spain

Of Spain's major makes, the Elizalde is surely the least known. Though it was marketed for 14 years from 1914, most of the cars were stolid fours in the 2-3-litre class, intended for domestic consumption. At the 1921 Paris Salon, however, the Barcelona firm showed a monstrous straight-eight.

Wheelbase was a formidable 169 inches (4·3 m), and under the towering bonnet lived an overhead-valve monobloc engine of 8·1 litres capacity, its twin horizontal carburetters fed by Autovac. The power – a figure of 150 bhp was quoted – was transmitted to the rear wheels via a cone clutch and a four-speed separate gearbox, the latter incorporating a power tyre pump. Springs were double half-elliptic all round, and there were two pedals for the servo-assisted brakes, one working on all four wheels, and the other on the front ones only. Dual ignition was fitted.

Understandably there were few takers, though a smaller and simpler 3·4-litre version was catalogued for several years.

Mathis P-Type

1922, France

The Strasbourg-based Mathis had been a German make before the Armistice of 1918, but after the war Émile Mathis set out to challenge France's Big Three – more especially Citroën. Though production built up to close on 20,000 cars a year by the later 1920s, he failed, probably through making too many models and laying overmuch stress on tiny, high-revving fours and sixes noted for fragile rear ends and healthy oil consumptions. One Mathis owner had to decarbonize his engine three times in 8,000 miles (13,000 km).

Typical of early Vintage offerings was the P-type illustrated, with a 760 cc four-cylinder side-valve monobloc engine. The magneto ignition and gravity feed were common practice in this class, while semi-elliptic springs and four forward speeds were assets lacking in contemporary Citroëns. There was, however, no differential, and foot and hand brakes worked on separate rear wheels. Factory claims of 55 mph (90 km/h) and 62 mpg (4·5 lit/100) were certainly optimistic.

One Spanish maker, Wilfredo Ricart of Pegaso, said that, as a poor country, Spain must make 'jewels for the rich'. This certainly applied to the huge Elizalde, though few foreign millionaires were tempted. Thus Elizalde stopped making cars by 1929.

For real economy-fiends there was the even smaller T, still a four-speeder, but weighing only 952 lb (430 kg). On this one, Mathis dispensed not only with a starter, but with electric lights as well.

Alongside the fours there was a range of pint-sized sixes using a similar chassis, also with splash lubrication and differential-less back axles, though unlike the P, these had Germanic vee-radiators. These light cars were discarded in 1927 in favour of the sedater M-type four.

Good weather protection, but poor visibility. This AC is actually a 1923 four-cylinder, but the same polished aluminium sports body was available on the 2-litre six.

AC 2-litre
1923, Great Britain

John Weller's overhead-camshaft AC Six must hold the record for longevity in car engines: unveiled at the 1919 London Show, it was still listed in 1963, by which time output had more than tripled the original 35 bhp. No wonder its makers boasted of 'The First Light Six–And Still the Finest'. It was also the first British car to win the Monte Carlo Rally outright, in 1926. In early years it was backed by that great publicist S. F. Edge, of pre-war Napier fame.

But though the engine's evolution was steady, the car in which it was installed in 1922 (when deliveries belatedly began) differed dramatically from the sophisticated Ace of the 1950s. The simple frame rode on quarter-elliptics, and the three-speed gearbox was mounted in unit with the worm-drive back axle, a component noted for unpleasing noises in the indirect ratios; it was as well that the Six was renowned for its top-gear flexibility. Fuel was fed by gravity from a dash tank–the filler was *inside* the cockpit–though the ineffectual disc handbrake of contemporary fours was not fitted to the 2-litre. The crankshaft was pressure-fed, and ignition was by magneto. Four-wheel brakes became available in 1925.

Edge's publicity stunts produced spectacular results. In 1924 a car recorded 34 mpg (8·3 lit/100) during top-gear trials; in 1925 Gillett drove solo at Montlhéry for 24 hours at a speed of 82·58 mph (132·13 km/h); and two years later the Bruces did 15,000 miles (24,000 km) at over 55 mph (90 km/h).

Austin's winged wheel badge.

Austin Seven
1923, Great Britain

The Austin Seven may not have been the world's first big car in miniature, but it was certainly one of the most successful. Average annual sales ran at over 20,000 for 11 of its 17 years of life. To the 300,000 cars built in Birmingham must be added licence production in Germany (BMW), France (Rosengart) and America (Bantam). Even after the last Baby Austin left Longbridge in the spring of 1939, its engine soldiered on in Reliant's three-wheelers until 1962. Japan's first Datsuns, if not direct copies, owed a great deal to the Austin.

Herbert Austin planned his miniature for a father, mother, and two children. It would be a civilized substitute for the motor-cycle and sidecar, which he termed 'an unmechanical contraption'. Thus all the virtues of a full-sized car would be condensed into a compact machine 104 inches (2·64 m) long and 46 inches (1·16 m) wide. The result was eminently successful, only the spidery wire wheels with their narrow-section tyres recalling earlier cyclecars.

The two-bearing, 747 cc side-valve four-cylinder engine developed 10 bhp; it featured thermo-siphon cooling, magneto ignition and splash lubrication. In unit with it were mounted the single-plate clutch and three-speed gearbox; gear and brake levers were central, while drive was by torque tube to a spiral bevel back end. The dash-mounted fuel tank held four gallons (20 litres) – sufficient for 200 miles (320 km). Suspension – by a transverse spring at the front and longitudinal quarter-elliptics at the rear – was inspired by Peugeot's 1919 Quadrilette. The frame was an A-shaped affair, open at the back. The four-wheel brakes, alas, had little more than publicity value: the drums were tiny, and they were uncoupled, so that both pedal and lever had to be used for crash stops. But at the £165 asked for a 'chummy' (tourer) it was excellent value, even if, like the much later Mini, it took some time to catch on. Deliveries would not break 10,000 a year until 1925.

Later variations were limitless. There was a whole flood of special bodies, notably William Lyons's first Swallow two-seaters and saloons, forerunners of the famed SS/Jaguar line. There were light vans, military derivatives, even a miniature taxicab. Catalogued sports models reached their zenith in 1930 with the supercharged Ulster, capable of 80 mph (128 km/h) on 33 bhp.

The Seven was also refined: 1922's mechanical starter was a very early casualty, but a speedometer was not standard equipment

▲*Electric starters were now standard, but the Austin Seven had undergone little further change by 1924. Note the tiny brake drums and the inadequate cowl-mounted head/side lamps.*

◀*Countless special-bodied Austin Sevens were offered alongside the factory's own styles. Very popular in 1927/28 was Gordon England's 'Cup' model with bulbous tail and flared wings. This coachbuilder was an early specialist in lightweight fabric styles. The degree of tune was usually up to the customer.*

until 1925. Saloon bodies were added to the range in 1926, two years later the combined head/side lamps were removed from the cowl to a more conventional location, and a coil replaced the magneto for 1929. In 1930 came coupled brakes (at last), from 1932 gearboxes acquired a fourth speed, and synchromesh arrived in 1934.

But refinement meant more weight. The delightful little 1923 Chummy illustrated opposite turned the scales at 728 lb (330 kg), but the 1935 Ruby saloon ran to a ponderous 1,358 lb (610 kg). True, it was faster than its ancestor, and still good for 45 mpg (6·3 lit/100), while its price, sliding roof and all, was a bargain £128. But by this time Ford and Morris had evolved more acceptable variations on a minimal theme.

The Austin Seven, however, remains a classic. One can forgive those uncertain brakes (even the coupled species were never very good) and the car's slightly old-maidish image for such idiosyncrasies as a clutch with its pedal travel measured in millimetres, the tinkle of the fixed starting handle, and the dashboard's dominant feature – a list of the patents incorporated in the car, which one infringed at one's peril.

Austro-Daimler ADM

1923, Austria

Austria's industry, like Belgium's, had a tough time in the 1920s. The country not only lost its captive home market through the carve-up of the Habsburg Empire: several major makers – Laurin-Klement, Nesselsdorf (Tatra) and Praga – fell to Czechoslovakia.

The Habsburg double-headed eagle outlived that dynasty in Austro-Daimler's badge. The mascot is an encircled bow and arrow.

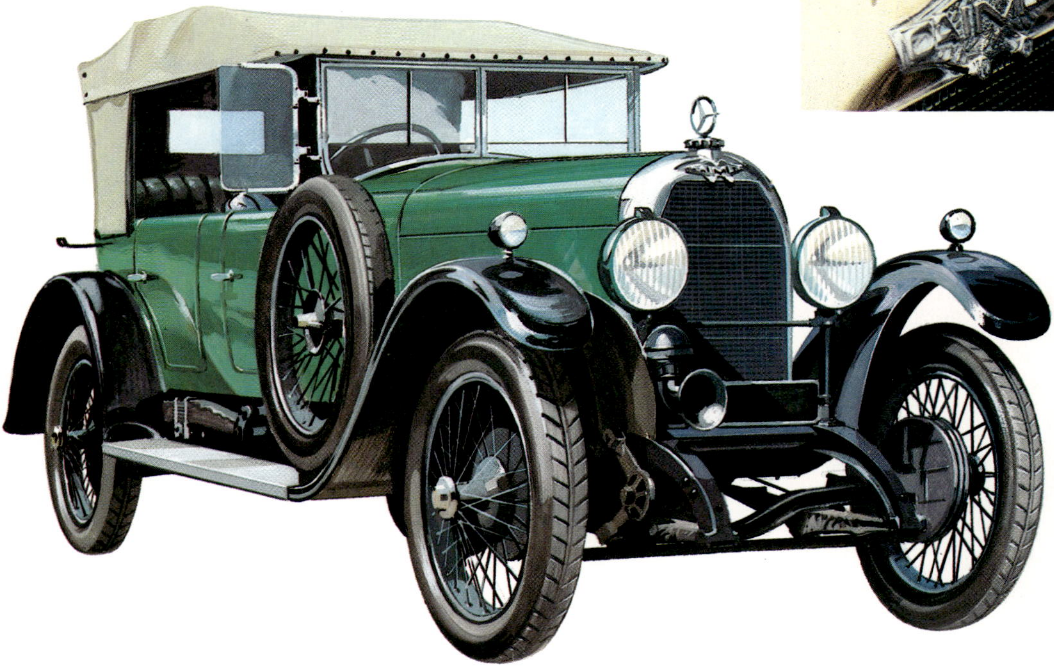

The Austro-Daimler dashboard, showing the instruments. To a modern driver the layout would seem very awkward.

For all the similarity of mascots, the German and Austrian Daimler companies were no longer connected, albeit Ferdinand Porsche designed for both in the 1920s. Before he left for Stuttgart, he gave the Viennese firm an excellent – and more economical – successor to the formidable chain-driven Prince Henry sports cars produced in the 1910–14 period.

Like the Prince Henry, the 1923 ADM wore its camshaft upstairs, but it was a $2\frac{1}{2}$-litre monobloc six with detachable head, disposing of a modest 50 bhp and intended for speeds of 60–65 mph (100–105 km/h). Block and pistons were of light alloy, and though there were only three main bearings, lubrication was of full-pressure type.

Magneto ignition and four forward speeds were to be expected, but insurances against central Europe's poor roads were the cantilever rear springs and the rigid mounting of the radiator on the engine. Wheels were centre-lock wire (balloon tyres came in 1925),

Hupmobile R

1923, United States

A 1923 Hupmobile coupé. Golf clubs would have been housed in the rear deck. The 'through-windscreen' spot lamp was a favourite period American accessory.

but the ADM had mechanical four-wheel brakes from the start.

After Porsche's departure, development was continued by Karl Rabe. A twin-carburetter sports edition offered 75 mph (120 km/h) in 1925, while even better was the 3-litre ADM3 (19/100 hp in Britain), good for 100 bhp and 100 mph (160 km/h) in short-chassis form and raced to some purpose in the later 1920s. The last six-cylinder Austro-Daimlers had servo brakes, tubular backbone frames and independently sprung rear ends; capacity went up to 3·6 litres. A merger with Steyr, though it saved the remnants of the Austrian industry, spelt the end for the Austro-Daimler. About 1,400 of the ADM/ADR sixes were made, the last of them in 1935/6.

Medium-sized independent concerns were still viable in America in 1923, though the Great Depression would be their death-knell. Hupmobile, who made all their own major elements, were still good for about 40,000 cars a year in 1923, even if they listed but a single model, and that a four uncomfortably close in specification to the popular Dodge. A touring Model-R cost $1,150 (£230) as against the $880 asked for its rival.

Like Dodge, Hupmobile did not believe in change for change's sake. The R had been around since 1917; it was a straightforward side-valve 3-litre with thermo-siphon cooling, vacuum feed, three-speed unit gearbox, dry multi-disc clutch, spiral bevel back end, all brakes on the rear wheels, and semi-elliptic springing. Wheelbase was 112 inches (2·845 m), and the full-pressure lubrication was a welcome refinement. Such improvements as had arrived by 1923 were principally cosmetic—a new radiator and the fashionable drum headlamps—though friction shock absorbers were now standard, and on home-market cars a coil replaced the earlier magneto. The 17 mpg (16 lit/100) thirst was reasonable in a land of cheap petrol.

For 1924, wheelbase went up to 115 inches (2·92 m), screenwipers were standardized, and the engine uprated from 35 to 40 bhp. There was also a smart close-coupled sedan in the catalogue, but fours were going out of fashion, and one-model ranges could no longer compete with line-ups such as those of General Motors or even Durant. A straight-eight Hupmobile was introduced in 1925, and a year later the old four gave way to a medium-sized six.

For their sports models, SPA, like Fiat and Itala, preferred aggressive vee-radiators.

SPA Tipo 24
1923, Italy

With a weak home market, Italy could afford only one super-car, the Isotta Fraschini: the V12s of Fiat and Lancia never saw production. SPA, however, tried harder, though trucks were always their principal interest and private car deliveries seldom achieved four figures a year.

Though smaller SPAs had four cylinders and side valves, Tipo 24 was more sophisticated, being a monobloc six with crossflow head, twin shaft-driven overhead camshafts, and dual ignition with 12 plugs (not to mention two separate ignition keys!). The three-bearing crankshaft was fully balanced, and pressure-fed; fuel supply was by Autovac. The four-speed unit gearbox had right-hand change, but the four-wheel brakes, for all their enormous drums, were uncoupled. The pedal worked on front wheels and transmission, and the lever on the rear. The latter was adequate for use at normal touring speeds.

Here was a really big car on a 147-inch (3·76m) wheelbase, turning the scales at two tonnes, and capable of over 80mph (130–135km/h). The truck image, however, did not help sales, and a bank failure in 1925 drove SPA into the arms of Fiat, who promptly discarded the private-car line.

Star Four
1923, United States

As an automobile, the Star is of no great interest. It represents the contemporary American norm for a cheap hack: splash-lubricated four-cylinder side-valve engine, pump cooling, coil ignition, vacuum feed, a three-speed gearbox driving to a spiral bevel back end, and a simple frame (admittedly with tubular backbone reinforcement) hung on semi-elliptic springs. Weight is a modest 1,750lb (795kg), and the car is good for a somewhat noisy 50mph (80km/h).

The vehicle's main interest is that it marked magnate William C. Durant's last bid for an empire. Twice he had headed General Motors, and twice he had been thrown out. Now he sought to challenge his old company with a full line of cars from this sub-utility offering in the Ford-Chevrolet market to the huge Locomobile 48 priced from $9,000 (£1,800) upward.

He tried hard. Like Chevrolet (though not, of course, Ford) his Star had a conventional transmission (publicity made much of the 'hand gear lever'), while prices were lower than Chevrolet's–$443 as against $495 for a fully equipped tourer. (Ford's similar package, however, cost only $380.) The catalogue even included a 'depot wagon', an early form of woody, or station wagon, at $610. In 1923, the make's first full year, the Durant Group sold 172,000 units.

But the going was heavy. Rival firms made almost everything themselves. Durant bought out–engines from Continental, gearboxes from Warner, electrics from Autolite. By 1927, overall sales were down to 80,000, and a year later the Star was discontinued.

1923 Vauxhall M-Type

Vauxhall M-Type
1923, Great Britain

In the tough economic climate of the early 1920s, even luxury-car makers were thinking of something smaller. In Britain, the horse-power tax was an additional headache. Vauxhall's regular D-type carried an annual impost of £25: hence C. E. King's M, new for 1922. This was a roomy car on a 114-inch (2·896 m) wheelbase, but annual tax was only £14, and list price, at £795, was lower than the usual Vauxhall levels, but admittedly higher than rival Rovers, Sunbeams and Arrol-Johnstons. The two latter makes were, however, taxed as sixteens.

Engineering was straightforward, with a pressure-lubricated, side-valve four-cylinder engine of 2·3 litres' capacity, pump cooling, magneto ignition, and a three-speed gearbox, still with right-hand change. Unusually on a Vauxhall, all brakes worked on the rear wheels. Four body styles were available in 1923, when the price was cut to £595.

Speeds of 55–60 mph (90–100 km/h) were possible, and in its later, LM guise (with four-speed box, front-wheel brakes and wire wheels) the 14/40 was well liked. The big factory was, however, under-employed (only 1,462 cars sold in 1923), and salvation came with a takeover by General Motors two years later. The result was, sadly, a swing towards the cheap and mass-produced.

The Star was one of the first factory-built station wagons. The seats were uncomfortable, and lateral protection was by roll-up side curtains. Ford would popularize the style on their 1929 Model-A.

1923 Star Four

Brooks
1924, Canada

To launch a new steam car in 1924 was brave enough; to do it in Canada was to tempt providence. The new venture was an updated Stanley with that make's late-type frontal condenser of 'radiator' shape. Also present were a vertical fire-tube boiler mounted under the bonnet, and a two-cylinder horizontal rear-mounted underfloor engine driving the back axle direct. The Stanley's full-elliptic springs had given way to half-elliptics, and all brakes were on the rear wheels. Controls were of Stanley type, with pedal-operated reverse and a thief-proof throttle lock. Brooks offered only one body, a four-door fabric sedan. This may have been their undoing, for with only a bulkhead between crew and boiler, cockpit temperatures must have been formidable.

The Brooks carried enough water for a range of 400 miles (600 km) and enough fuel for 250 miles (400 km). Nobody, however, wanted steam cars at the Packard price of $3,885 (£775), and the firm's bid for a captive market with their own taxi company got them nowhere. In 1927 it was reported that 180 cars had been sold, but despite a $1,000 price reduction, 40 brand-new machines were still on hand a year later when the plant was sold up. Some of these cars fetched only $150 (£30) at auction.

Chrysler 70
1924, United States

The original Chrysler 70 was a landmark in more ways than one. It was the first product of a new empire that would soon rank third in the American industry, behind General Motors and Ford. It was also an outstanding performer for its day. American motorists had been accustomed to top speeds in the low 50s (80–85 km/h), with a cruising gait of perhaps 40 (60 km/h): the Chrysler was capable of an honest 70 (120 km/h), and cruised at 60. Better still, not only did it have a brake on each wheel, but these anchors were hydraulically actuated. The fact that they were still of the dirt-prone contracting type did not matter unduly at a time when this system was accepted practice. Chrysler's handbrake worked on the transmission, and would continue so to do until the 1960s.

Walter P. Chrysler had graduated via top management at General Motors to being a manufacturer in his own right through the purchase of the Maxwell-Chalmers combine. Neither firm was in good shape, either financially or technically, but production continued while Chrysler's 'Three Musketeers' – Carl Breer, Owen Skelton, and Fred Zeder – worked out their new creation.

Its engine was startling enough. Though still a side-valve six, it was of high-compression type, giving 68 bhp from 3·3 litres at a brisk

1924 Brooks

Walter P. Chrysler with his masterpiece, a 1924 70 two-door sedan. Fixed wood wheels and demountable rims still predominated in America. Spare wheels were, however, usually rear-mounted: a side-mount as on this car was exceptional.

The Chrysler badge.

1924 Chrysler 70

3,200 rpm – 2,400 was then the normal rate of rotation for an American touring unit. The crankshaft was pressure-lubricated and ran to seven main bearings, though, the brakes apart, there was nothing else heretical about the Chrysler. The coil ignition, vacuum feed, spiral bevel back axle, and semi-elliptic springs with friction dampers differed not at all from other American offerings.

Performance, however, was inexpensive. The touring cost $1,335 (£267) and it was only one of eight body styles, even if hardly any of the costly ($3,725) Formal Town Cars found buyers. In Britain, the smart open roadsters acquired the image of a 'poor man's Bentley', a reputation reinforced by a seventh place at Le Mans in 1925, and an even more startling third place three years later.

Sales rose dramatically, from 32,000 in 1924 to 76,600 in 1925 and to 162,242 in 1926. Of the older makes, the Chalmers, as direct competition, had been phased out during 1924; the Maxwell hung on another year before giving way to a four-cylinder Chrysler. 1926 would see some more powerful sixes, an improved 3·6-litre 70 and the 4·7-litre Imperial 80, developing 92 bhp and capable of cruising at 75 mph (120 km/h). By the end of 1928 Walter Chrysler had absorbed the old-established Dodge concern. He had also launched two cheaper makes, the Plymouth Four and the De Soto Six, which gave him a market coverage that was comparable to that of General Motors.

De Dion-Bouton IW

1924, France

De Dions being readied for sale by the English importers in 1924. The two-seater 'doctor's coupé' was a popular style. De Dion advertised bodies tailored to individual requirements, in England at any rate.

The once-great house of de Dion-Bouton had run out of ideas by 1924. Their product was well made, but it was not cheap enough to compete with Renault, nor individual and fast enough to challenge the new generation of 2-litre fast tourers like the Delage. Even such endearing idiosyncrasies as the pre-war decelerator pedal had gone. Instead the company's mainstay was a line of 1·8-litre fours with pressure lubrication, 12-volt electrics (de Dion made their own magnetos) and cantilever rear springs. With their vee-radiators, optional-extra wire wheels, and the convertible bodies offered by the British importers, they were handsome, but good looks alone could not sell a ponderous 2,500-pounder (about 1,100 kg) capable of a leisurely 45 mph (72 km/h).

There was variety enough. The 1·8-litre de Dions came as ISs, with rear-wheel brakes, side valves, and 24 bhp; the IT was the same thing with front-wheel brakes. The IV was an IS with overhead valves, detachable head, and wire wheels, and the IW was an IT similarly uprated.

The overhead-valve cars were at least a little faster, while some improvements were made, 1924's principal novelty being vacuum instead of gravity feed. Front-wheel brakes were standardized in 1925, but an IW still cost half as much again as a Citroën tourer in France.

De Dion tried hard, with a simple 1·3-litre model selling for under £200 in England, but in 1926 this was too late, and soon after came the first of a series of financial crises which would bring private-car production to a halt in 1932.

Delage DI

1924, France

One of the most attractive types of car popular in the 1920s was the 2-litre fast tourer. This was not a sports car, though often treated as one by its owners, who ordered it with sporting open bodywork. Ballot, Delage and Schneider in France, Lagonda in England, and Lancia and OM in Italy were among the leading exponents of this theme. Four cylinders and overhead valves were the norm, though exceptionally the OM was a flathead six.

Delage's DI family were among the most successful of their generation, with total sales of nearly 11,000 units in five seasons, a creditable performance for a car selling at over £650 ($3,250) in Britain. The four cylinders had the classical dimensions of 75 × 120 mm (2,121 cc), and there were overhead valves in a detachable head. Cooling was by thermo-siphon and buyers had a choice of magneto or coil ignition: starting was by a dynamotor driven off the nose of the five-bearing crank-shaft. The four-speed gearbox had central change, allowing of either left- or right-hand steering, though the latter was commoner, even in France.

Chassis design was orthodox, with semi-elliptic springs, friction dampers, and a spiral bevel back axle. The cable-operated four-wheel brakes were actuated by lever and pedal alike, with the optional of servo assist-ance. The frame was robust, with five cross-members.

The standard car was good for about 65 mph (105 km/h), a gallon of fuel lasting 22 miles (13·2 lit/100). The 126-inch (3·2-m) wheelbase permitted the fitting of heavy closed coachwork, and there was even a Colonial model with raised ground clearance. For enthusiasts Delage offered the DIS and DISS, with tuned engines, bigger oil pumps, lowered frames, and close-ratio gearboxes. These managed about 75 mph (120 km/h) and looked their best with boat-tail two- and four-seater bodies.

Unfortunately a growing demand for flexi-bility led to the DI's abandonment in 1928 in favour of the uninteresting DR, a side-valve six. No more sporting fours would emerge from this factory.

The Delage in more elegant sports guise. This car wears later well-base rims to take modern tyres.

1924 Delage DI

Lanchester 21

1924, Great Britain

In pre-1914 days the Lanchester brothers had been the individualists *par excellence* of automobile design. Their cars incorporated forward control, preselective epicyclic gearboxes, wick carburetters, and silent worm drive. Only the last feature, however, was found on 1924's 21 hp: convention and a commercially-minded board of directors had moved in.

The underslung worm drive permitted a low body line. Other Lanchester characteristics were the sight glass in the radiator header tank, and the construction of the factory-built bodies with their aluminium framing and rubber mounts. Panelling was of course also in light alloy. The rest of the car was, however, orthodox: the eight-bearing 3-litre overhead-camshaft six-cylinder engine was pressure-lubricated, but in place of the old epicyclic box was a four-speed sliding type with right-hand change, though Lanchester's cantilever rear springing, with its first-class ride, was retained.

Wheelbase, at 129 inches (3·28 m), was identical to that of the Rolls-Royce 20 announced a year earlier. The Lanchester was planned as a direct competitor, selling in chassis form for £50 less. Further, it offered several advantages – more power, at 59 bhp as against 50, and therefore more speed, not to mention four forward speeds and the front-wheel brakes which its rival as yet lacked. There was also the kudos of royal patronage: the Duke of York (George VI) supplemented his 40-hp Lanchester with one of the smaller cars in 1926, by which time capacity had been increased to 3·3 litres. To the Rolls-Royce's credit were slightly higher standards of flexibility and silence, one of the reasons why Henry Royce did not use overhead-camshaft engines. But despite the Lanchester's slightly longer production run, it sold only 716 cars to the Rolls-Royce's 2,940.

A Lanchester saloon body before painting, showing some of the aluminium frame. Unlike most of their rivals, the firm built most of their own coachwork.

The Lanchester's radiator header tank with sight glass, inherited from pre-war days.

Locomobile 48

1924, United States

Even in the United States pre-war designs lingered on into the mid-1920s. Alongside the Packard and Duesenberg straight-eights, Locomobile of Bridgeport, Connecticut (by now the prestige division of the Durant group) offered their 8·6-litre 48, with an ancestry going back to 1909. If one ignored the full electrics, the under-bonnet scene recalled the Brass Age, with six huge pair-cast cylinders and the antiquated T-head valve gear incorporating two side camshafts. Even the angular radiator shell suggested a 1914 Mercedes.

The car was built on an heroic scale – wheelbase was 142 inches (3·62 m), frame side-members were 6 inches (15·2 cm) deep, and the threequarter-elliptic rear springs 50 inches (1·25 m) long. Open cars weighed around 5,000 lb 2,300 kg), and the engine developed its 95 bhp at a lazy 2,200 rpm. Fuel was fed from a 30-gallon (150-litre) rear tank by air pressure, and there was dual ignition with two sets of spark plugs. While left-hand drive and central control had come as long ago as 1915, Locomobile, almost alone among American makers, clung to four forward speeds and 12-volt electrics. Two spare tyres, a spotlamp, and a power tyre pump were inclusive in prices starting at around the $8,000 (£1,600) mark. Locomobile designed and built their own bodies, some of which had an ageless elegance. The Sportif, a sporting tourer listed in 1924, gave no evidence of its 1915–16 origins.

In 1924 the 48 was available with balloon tyres and four-wheel brakes; it was also still selling at the rate of 400–500 a year. It would, however, soon be joined by a medium-priced straight-eight to challenge the new Chrysler, and 1926 saw a smaller L-head monobloc six – only 6 litres this time – for the carriage trade. Sales of this one in its first season were a meagre 184 units. As for the 48, deliveries were down to a trickle, though the aged giant would still be available when Locomobile finally closed their doors in 1929.

A Locomobile Town Car in Hollywood. The absence of front-wheel brakes indicates pre-1924. Noteworthy are the distinctive headlamps.

1924 Locomobile 48

Trojan PB

1924, Great Britain

Automobile design may have been stereotyped in the United States, and fast settling into a similar mould in the Old World, but some real eccentricities were still marketed – and sold – in the 1920s. Only about 15,000 Trojan cars found buyers between 1922 and 1929, but the vehicle was immensely popular as a light van.

The first impression one gained of the Trojan was that nothing was where one expected it to be. The car had an orthodox bonnet and radiator, but only the latter was functional; the former was empty save for the fuel tank and carburetter. The engine was mounted horizontally amidships under the floorboards. It was a watercooled, four-cylinder 'duplex' $1\frac{1}{2}$-litre two-stroke in which each pair of cylinders shared a common combustion chamber and sparking plug. Lubrication was of petroil type, and ignition was by coil. This unit lived in a punt-shaped, pressed-steel frame, and drove rearwards via a two-speed epicyclic gearbox and roller chain. There was no differential.

Nor was the catalogue of eccentricity exhausted. Inspection of the cockpit revealed two right-hand levers: one selected the gears, but the other, of pull-up type, actuated a mechanical starter. There was no electrical device to mar a Trojan's simplicity. Brakes were on the rear axle and transmission, while the easy ride of the long cantilever springs was exploited by designer Leslie Hounsfield, to dispense with the puncture menace. Trojans rode on solid tyres, though pneumatics were an optional extra.

Of styling there was none. However bodied (saloons were available from 1928), the car was uncompromisingly ugly. An ingenious feature was the transparent rear number plate, illuminated by the tail lamp. A slot was cut in the rear panel for the convenience of the absent-minded!

Hounsfield's dream was a foolproof people's car. He had been testing prototypes (mechanically similar, but with forward control) since 1910. The design was adopted in 1922 by Leyland for manufacture in their Kingston-upon-Thames factory. The Trojan was astonishingly durable: if driving chains required replacement at 20,000-mile (32,000-km) intervals, engines lasted 100,000 miles (160,000 km) or more, and never needed decarbonizing. Further, the modest 10 bhp was available throughout the power curve, and the reward for 1905-style performance (32 mph, or 51 km/h) was the ability to climb anything on which the wheels could find a grip. Trojan advertising chose the brilliant punchline 'Can You Afford to Walk?'. A true assessment came from the late Arthur Scroggs, perhaps the most dedicated Trojanist of all time: the car, he said, 'did what it was intend-

◄ *Trojans developed the same power at any engine speed, and were thus ideal for steep hills. This cross-country six-wheeler was tried in 1927. It wears the optional Trojan's Head mascot. Similar cars were supplied to the South African army.*

► *The 1930 RE Trojan carried its engine – still a two-stroke – vertically behind the rear axle, and offered three forward speeds instead of two. The spare wheel was fixed on a swinging bracket outside the engine compartment, not inside as this photograph suggests.*

Trojan beginnings: one of the prototypes tested by Leslie Hounsfield in 1913–14. It looks very different from the production PB, mainly because Hounsfield took full advantage of the unorthodox engine location under the seat and gave his car semi-forward control, as on early Lanchesters. The wood-spoke wheels give this first Trojan an archaic appearance, as do the oil lamps. But the four-cylinder, two-stroke engine, two-speed epicyclic box, and chain drive were the same as on production models.

1924 Trojan PB

ed to do most efficiently, but it was designed to do what very few people wanted'.

Herein lay the rub. Garages loathed it: 'No Trojans' notices were commonplace in the 1920s. In days when Austin Sevens and Morris-Cowleys cruised comfortably at 35 mph (55 km/h), there was no future for a car that could not achieve such a velocity on full throttle. Leyland pulled out in 1928, leaving Trojan dependent on their small shops at Croydon. Trojan sought to bring their ideas up to date with a modern-looking rear-engined saloon, but this RE had lost all the old virtues and acquired some new vices – notably overheating – on the way. After 1936, the company concentrated on commercial vehicles, though they were still fitting two-stroke fours, albeit front-mounted and wedded to a conventional driveline, as late as the mid-50s.

Adler 6/25 PS

1925, Germany

By 1925, German manufacturers were making determined attempts to catch up. Relatively prosperous were Adler of Frankfurt, who had a useful business in typewriters as well. Their triangular badge suggested affinities with the similarly-adorned American Hudson, but such Hudson influences as there were began with the Becker designs of the later 1920s. The 6/25 illustrated above was typical of European $1\frac{1}{2}$-litre machinery, its alloy pistons and connecting-rods apart.

The engine was a straightforward monobloc side-valve four with pressure lubrication (not found on Hudsons) and three main bearings, cooled by thermosiphon. The gravity feed, single-plate clutch, and semi-elliptic suspension were to be expected, though the four-wheel brakes, of contracting type, were a little ahead of the rest: Citroëns and Morris-Cowleys still lacked them, and they were extra on Fiat's 501. The 12-volt electrics and four forward speeds represented advanced thinking. Central change, though not left-hand steering, was featured.

Sales of 6,500 cars in just over four seasons reflected a weak market, and by 1929 American influence had moved in. The 6/25's 2-litre successor featured coil ignition and vacuum feed. Brakes were internal-expanding hydraulic, but the four-speed box had given way to a three-speeder.

The Doble brothers in their first prototype, 1912.

Doble kept his boiler under the bonnet.

1925 Doble E

The little Hanomag was also offered as an open two-seater.

Doble E
1925, United States

Although only 42 of Abner Doble's magnificent steam cars found buyers, they eliminated the twin endemic bugbears of the system: the slow fire-up from cold, and an inability to cope with sustained high speeds.

Doble used electric ignition, with a sparking plug in the base of the combustion chamber, and an electric fan to feed air to the atomizer. Thus the Model-E, illustrated opposite, could be under way in three minutes. With a water capacity sufficient for 1,500 miles (24,000 km), an easy 70 mph (112 km/h) could be held indefinitely, with the engine turning silently at 900 rpm. The Stanley configuration was of course used, with the flash-type boiler under the bonnet, and the four-cylinder double-acting compound engine direct-coupled to the back axle, with no gearbox interposed. Wear was negligible, the engine being guaranteed for 100,000 miles (160,000 km).

The frame, of 142-inch (3·62 m) wheelbase, had seven tubular cross-members: later Dobles had four-wheel brakes. Controls were simple – two pedals regulating the valves and one for the brakes, plus a wheel within the steering wheel (this, incidentally, was of African ebony with a German silver spider) to open and close the throttle.

Murphy of Pasadena did the bodies, and customers included Howard Hughes and Bebe Daniels. There was only one fatal snag – even a bare chassis cost $6,800 (£1,360), with complete-car prices starting at $8,000. And this at a time when one could buy a straight-eight Packard for less than half the money.

Hanomag Kommissbrot
1925, Germany

A German light car with all-independent springing, platform frame, and rear engine? One thinks instantly of the Volkswagen, yet such a vehicle was on sale in 1925, seven years before the 'Beetle''s first recognized prototype took the road. What is more, nearly 16,000 of Hanomag's Kommissbrot – slang for the German Army loaf and a dig at the car's slab-sided appearance – found buyers in three years.

The shape was aimed at giving maximum elbow room on a vehicle 46½ inches (1·18 m) wide. The car came in open and closed forms, the latter also being used as a mini-taxi. Front suspension was by double transverse springs, with coils at the rear. The engine was a vertical overhead-valve single of 499 cc, mounted across the frame ahead of its radiator; the fan drive actually went through the core. Drive was transmitted through a three-speed gearbox and a roller chain to a differential-less axle. Both gearchange and steering-wheel were on the right, and both brakes worked on the rear wheels. Like the Trojan, the Hanomag featured a pull-up mechanical starter in the cockpit; electric starting was optional. A single cyclops-eye headlamp lived in the curved nose panel. The car weighed 816 lb (just under 370 kg), and would do 40 mph (60 km/h).

In 1928 the Kommissbrot gave way to a conventionally sprung light car with front vertical four-cylinder engine. Thereafter the Hanover factory displayed no more heretical tendencies, though it marketed one of the first diesel private cars in 1937.

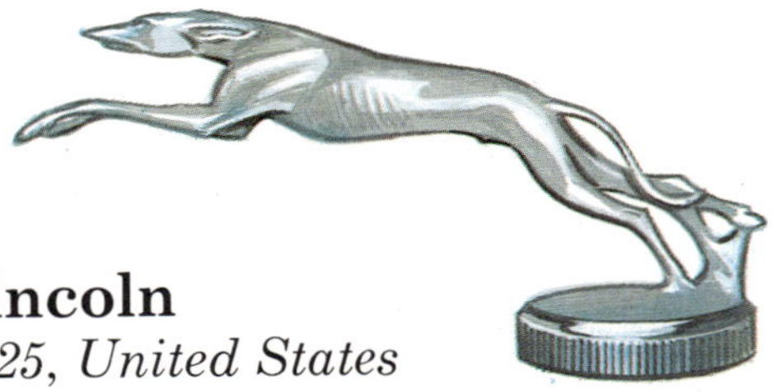

Lincoln

1925, United States

The Lincoln was Henry Ford's luxury line, and the preferred transport of American Presidents from Harding onward. Its speed endeared it to cops and robbers alike, though only the former could specify front-wheel brakes before 1927.

The car was, of course, the brainchild of Henry and Wilfred Leland of Cadillac fame, and was made in their own factory after they left General Motors. Like the Cadillac, the car was a side-valve V8, though the blocks were at a narrower angle (60 degrees rather than 90) to each other. Cylinder heads were detachable, and full-pressure lubrication was used. For the rest, specification was conventional, with pump cooling, a three-speed gearbox, a spiral bevel rear axle, and a channel-section frame riding on semi-elliptic springs. On 90bhp it was a good performer, but spoilt by the stodgy appearance of its Murray-built bodies. Henry Leland, as an engineer, had no interest in styling. This and his perfectionism led to heavy losses, and the company sold out to Henry Ford in 1922, after just over 3,700 cars had been delivered.

Under Ford ownership there was no loss in quality – and no dramatic change either. Hydraulic dampers were added in 1924, but under Edsel Ford's supervision Lincolns acquired an elegance hitherto absent. The vertical (instead of horizontal) radiator shutters were an improvement, while all bodies ordered by the factory had to have Edsel's personal approval. Sales climbed, from 5,512 in 1922 to 7,053 in 1924 and to over 8,000 in 1925, this despite prices slightly higher than Packard's and appreciably above Cadillac levels. In 1924, a Cadillac touring cost $3,085, a Packard $3,650 and the Lincoln $3,800.

But Lincolns were fast. A sedan weighing $2\frac{1}{2}$ tons managed 68mph (109km/h), and would accelerate from 10 to 60mph (16–98km/h) in 41 seconds. With open bodywork the car was appreciably faster.

1925 Lincoln

Sizaire Frères 4RI

1925, France

Maurice Sizaire had been a pioneer of advanced suspensions. As early as 1905 he had created the Sizaire-Naudin light car with independent front springing by transverse leaf. In 1923 he showed a new design on which the rear wheels were independently sprung as well.

In essence this was a 2-litre fast tourer competitive with the DI Delage (pages 38–9), though Sizaire's four-cylinder engine was a more powerful overhead-camshaft affair with two main bearings, and his three-speed gearbox suffered from noisy indirects. Like the Delage, the Sizaire featured vacuum feed and mechanical four-wheel brakes, but here all resemblance ceased. Sizaire's chassis was a narrow double backbone with deep side-members, while a combination of transverse springs and lower wishbones was used at either end. Steering was by rack and pinion.

There were other ingenious features. The brake cables were insulated from dirt in aluminium conduits, and the handbrake worked on the front wheels if pushed on, and on the rear if pulled back. The radiator, of Rolls-Royce shape, was a legacy of the Anglo-French Sizaire-Berwick, which Maurice had created in 1913.

The superb handling could not, however, cancel out the effect of shaky finances, and only 900 4RIs were sold. A 16-valve supercharged version failed through inherent crankshaft weakness, and the last Sizaires were sixes using the American Willys-Knight sleeve-valve engine. Between 1930 and 1934 some further cars were made under licence in Belgium.

Maurice Sizaire used his publicity to emphasize his car's excellent ride, and here a sporting torpedo is seen at speed under rugged conditions. The artist has laid great stress on the transverse springing at the front.

The Sizaire brothers' monogram forms the centre of their badge.

Davis 92

1926, United States

'Built of the Best' was Davis's slogan. It was a wholly assembled car, using bought-out bits from well-known proprietary firms—Continental engine, Borg and Beck clutch, Timken axles. It sold better than many rivals (3,000 in 1922) and lasted longer, being still quoted in 1930. There were even plans to make it under licence in Winnipeg for the Canadian market, but the few cars sold were fully imported.

In 1926 form the Davis was undistinguished in specification and appearance. Its 3·8-litre side-valve Continental six engine was shared by Peerless and Jewett, and gave 63 bhp. Cooling was by pump, and there were the usual three-speed gearbox, vacuum feed and spiral bevel rear end. The only unusual features were the full-detachable disc wheels and the contracting-type four-wheel hydraulic brakes, as yet used by one big-volume producer only: Chrysler. Wheelbase was 115 inches (2·92 m), and the sedan price was $1,595, about midway between what was asked for Buick's two sixes, the Standard and the Master. There were five body styles, the sportier ones bearing attractive labels such as 'Legionaire' and 'Man o'War'. Davises were seldom seen outside their homeland.

Hillman 14

1926, Great Britain

Before the establishment of the Rootes Group and the birth of the Minx (1932) the Hillman was neither commonly seen nor very well known, though cars had been made since 1907, and their 1913 light car had sold quite well.

1926 Hillman 14

The 2-litre 14 of 1926 was regarded by the public as a less usual and faster alternative to the familiar Austin 12.

Superficially, the two cars were not dissimilar. Both were side-valve fours with magneto ignition, single-plate clutches, and four-speed unit gearboxes. Both had four-wheel mechanical brakes, and other chassis features, even down to the 112-inch (2·845 m) wheelbase, ran parallel. The Hillman's vacuum feed was more sophisticated, while traditionalists preferred its right-hand change to the Austin's central lever. Further, the Hillman was cheaper—£295 for a tourer when the comparable Austin listed at £340.

With only three main bearings, the Hillman never gained quite the Austin's reputation for indestructibility, and the early angular saloon bodies were very ugly, though more rounded lines were seen in 1927. Refinements in 1928 included servo brakes and safety glass on the de-luxe line, while 1929s and 1930s resembled miniature Humbers. Sales, however, told their own story: between 1926 and 1928 the public bought nearly 40,000 Austins but only about 7,500 Hillmans.

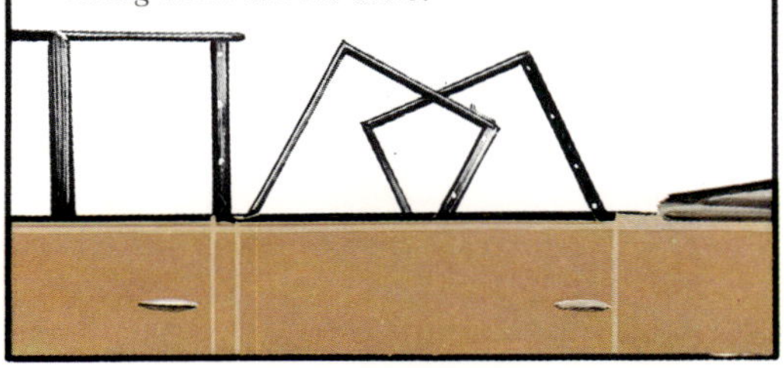

Saloon-car refinement in an open tourer. How Humber's rigid and weather-proof side-curtains swung down into the doors.

Humber 9/20 hp

1926, Great Britain

Humber's post-war light cars were the sort of machinery that sold well only in Britain: small-capacity tourers constructed to the highest standards. The firm claimed that the rigid side curtains supplied on their open cars offered saloon-type weather protection, but the marginal motorist in search of a bargain in 1926 would not have chosen the 9/20 for all its refinement. At £260, it was undercut not only by Morris and Clyno, but also by Rover's 9/20 (£190) and by the imported 509 Fiat at £215.

None the less, the little car sold well, accounting for nearly half the 3,306 new Humbers made that year. The model's roots lay in the company's first post-war baby, the 985 cc 8/18 seen at the 1922 London Show. This had a two-bearing monobloc four-cylinder engine with overhead inlet valves, splash lubrication and (surprisingly) coil ignition, though a magneto was used from 1924. The clutch was a cone, three forward speeds sufficed, and the footbrake worked (not very well) on the transmission. Springs were quarter-elliptic.

This car had grown up by 1926 into the 1,056 cc 9/20 on a longer wheelbase with room for four-seater bodies. It also featured semi-elliptic suspension, a rear tank with Autovac feed, and a front-wheel brake option, albeit of uncoupled type, and retaining the old drum on the transmission.

Morris-Cowley

1926, Great Britain

Not a few manufacturers are forced into assembling proprietary bits when the cash runs out, but the reversal of the process is rare. It happened to William Richard Morris, and it made him a millionaire as well as the maker of Britain's best-selling car. A total of 54,151 Morrises found buyers in 1925, and over 32,000 in 1926 despite a major model change.

Morris had two economic weapons. The first was his courage in reducing prices in the teeth of slump and inflation. In 1920 his inexpensive two-seater Cowley was not selling at £465, but a year later it was going great guns at a mere £299. By the end of 1923 the price was down below £200, and in 1926 the same article, complete with optional-extra front brakes, retailed at £170.

To keep pace with a demand destined to give him 41 per cent of the home market by 1925, Morris bought up the component suppliers on whom he had hitherto been dependent – Osberton (radiators), Hollick and Pratt (bodies), Wrigley (transmissions), and Hotchkiss of Coventry (engines). Thus what had been just another assembled light car in 1921 became a fully manufactured object four years later, even if the main plant at Cowley

1926 Morris-Cowley

This modern photograph of a 1926 Morris-Cowley saloon shows the absence of doors on the driver's side, leaving plenty of room for spare wheel, battery box and spare can of fuel.

A factory shot of possibly the first-ever Pontiac with a load of apprehensive executives. They need not have worried, however: the car was an immediate success.

Pontiac's Indian Head mascot, commemorating the famous 18th-century Ottawa chief.

was solely concerned with putting the pieces together.

The Morris-Cowley had started life in 1915 as a mixture of American-built components, by Continental, Detroit Gear, and Timken. It was a simple side-valve $1\frac{1}{2}$-litre four, cooled by thermo-siphon and blessed with a sweet, wet-plate clutch, this and the three-speed box being of unit construction. A central gear-change was used, rear springs were three-quarter elliptic, and in 1926, its final 'Bullnose' year, the car featured a five-lamp lighting set, silent dynamotor starting, friction dampers, balloon tyres, and the four-wheel brake option. The result was a reliable hack, backed by nationwide service, and capable of 50 mph (80 km/h) and 28 mpg (10·2 lit/100). Prices started at £162·50, and a light van edition was also offered.

Somehow, however, the flatnose cars made from 1927 onwards never had the 'Bullnose's' character, though the Cowley continued to sell briskly until it was dropped at the end of 1934.

Pontiac Six

1926, United States

Still in production in 1980, and a safe bet for the top five in the American sales race, the Pontiac was the result of a General Motors plan to fill a gap in their price-structure between the utilitarian Chevrolet and the Oakland. Five years passed between the start of the project and its fruition in 1926, while initially the breed was a cheap companion make to the Oakland. Its role as a 'junior line' was, however, of short duration. In the Pontiac's first year, it outsold Oakland by a cool 20,000; the ratio was 3-to-1 in Pontiac's favour in 1927, and by the end of 1931 the Oakland was no more.

The new make was by no means a technical breakthrough. The 1926 Pontiac was little more than a lengthened Chevrolet chassis using a side-valve six instead of Chevrolet's overhead-valve four. Engineering was copy-book American: by now one expected full pressure lubrication on a new design, but the single-plate clutch, three-speed gearbox, and wood wheels with demountable rims were no surprise. On a sedan selling for around the $800 (£160) mark, four-wheel brakes were a needless luxury, and initially only closed bodies were offered. By an engaging quirk of publicity, the first Pontiac off the line was also GM's five millionth car.

The basic 110-inch (2·8-m) wheelbase type with 3-litre engine ran for several seasons, acquiring four-wheel brakes in 1928, while a year later output was up to 57 bhp. By this time, too, a full line of seven body styles was offered.

Steyr Type XII
1926, Austria

While Austro-Daimler produced luxury sporting cars in Austria, Steyr catered for a middle-class clientele. They were an ordnance firm new to the industry, but they could also draw on distinguished designers like Hans Ledwinka and Ferdinand Porsche. The first Steyr was a big overhead-camshaft six. Such expensive machinery, however, relied too heavily on export sales, which explains the advent of the 1·6-litre model, illustrated below, at the 1925 shows.

The six-cylinder monobloc engine with its chain-drive overhead camshaft was a legacy from earlier cars, but this one weighed only 2,215 lb (1,000 kg) in tourer form. The crankshaft ran in three ball bearings, cooling was by pump, and early examples had magneto ignition. Austria's mountainous road conditions were reflected in low axle ratios (there was a 6·3/1 option!) and a four-speed gearbox, as well as in four-wheel brakes with servo assistance and big (13 in, or 33 cm, diameter) drums.

Most interesting of all was the suspension – semi-elliptic at the front, but independent at the rear, by an arrangement of swing axles and coils that later became familiar on Mercedes-Benz of the 1930s. On Type XIIs, the engineers even dispensed with shock absorbers. This mixed springing would later be applied to the big Austro-Daimlers, giving alarming results in the wet, but it was well matched to the sedate Steyr with its 53 mph (85 km/h) top speed.

Like Lancia, Steyr offered a detachable top for tourer bodies, which posed storage problems; fabric saloon versions sold better. Over 11,000 Type XIIs found buyers, and until the Austrian bank crash of 1930 the model helped keep Steyr's annual deliveries around the 4,000 mark.

1926 Steyr Type XII

Steyr's 'target' emblem was appropriate for a firm also making small arms.

Stutz AA
1926, United States

Not all American cars followed the uniform pattern laid down by the mass-producers and by assemblers such as Davis (page 48). The Stutz eight, brainchild of C. R. Greuter, was different in most ways.

True, styling was stodgy, and many a familiar feature was to be seen – vacuum feed, a single-plate clutch, and semi-elliptic springs – but Stutz, like Lanchester, favoured an underslung worm drive to keep the centre of gravity low, and dual coil ignition was provided. Further, the 4·7-litre straight-eight engine had a robust nine-bearing crankshaft, while the overhead valves, remarkable in themselves, were actuated by a chain-

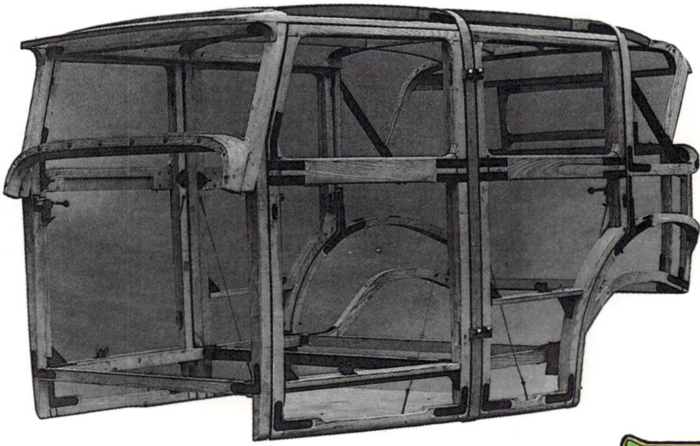

The lightweight skeleton of a Weymann flexible fabric body as used by Stutz in the late 1920s.

The Egyptian god Ra became the Stutz mascot with the introduction of the eight-cylinder line in 1926.

The Stutz badge, like the Ra mascot, reflects an Ancient Egyptian style.

1926 Stutz AA

driven overhead camshaft. Thus output was a useful 92 bhp. There was no loss of flexibility: the AA Stutz would accelerate from a walking pace in top to its maximum of 80 mph (128 km/h).

Less reliable were the hydraulic brakes, largely because on 1926–7 models they used a 50–50 alcohol/water mixture as fluid. 1928's orthodox Lockheeds were much more predictable. The AA also featured a primitive form of safety glass, in the form of a wire-impregnated sandwich, which helped to reinforce the 'Safety Stutz' label attached by the press department. Alone among American makers, Stutz were addicted to Weymann fabric bodies, found on many sedans and coupés of the period.

Performance and roadholding were exceptional. By 1927 the Black Hawk speedsters with high-ratio back ends were good for 105 mph (168 km/h) on 125 bhp, and a year later the stock power unit gave 125 bhp from 4·9 litres. Stutz's second place at Le Mans in 1928 gave the Bentleys a fright, and by 1932 the company had a 5·2-litre twin-cam model in production. This offered over 100 mph (160 km/h) in standard form, but the Indianapolis factory would be yet another victim of the Great Depression.

Fiat 509A

1927, Italy

Fiat's—and Italy's—first cheap baby car for world markets was introduced late in 1924. It was almost a national event, backed by the company's first internally-financed time-payments scheme.

It also marked the final phase in a transformation of Fiat's image, as well as a commentary on European ideas in inexpensive family cars. Up to 1908 Fiat had built big machines of Mercedes type for the carriage trade. The first step towards something more modest had come in 1908 with Tipo 1, a 2-litre four popular as a taxi. Next, in 1912, came the Zero, with a speed of nearly 50 mph (80 km/h) from 1·8 litres, but still costing £375 in England. The $1\frac{1}{2}$-litre 501 of 1919 achieved a production run of 80,000 in nine seasons, but it was still a relatively expensive car, selling for over £300 even in 1925. Now a real miniature had arrived.

The Fiat factory in Turin backs onto the Alps, and the new 509 was obviously mountain-bred. This was reflected in the mechanical four-wheel brakes standardized from the start, and also in the combination of a high-revving engine (the 990 cc four developed its 20 bhp at 3,800 rpm) and low gearing—the highest ratio of the three-speed box was 6 to 1.

The overhead-camshaft power unit featured magneto ignition and pressure lubrication, and electrics were 12-volt. Steel artillery wheels were used. Fuel was fed by gravity from a dash tank. Since right-hand steering was logical for mountain work, Fiat kept it on their new baby to the end in 1929. As for styling, the old pearshaped radiator had gone in favour of the angular, Rolls-Royce idiom initiated by Isotta Fraschini and Lancia, and imitated by the rest of the Italian industry. By 1927 it was hard to tell a small Fiat from a comparable Bianchi except by opening the bonnet.

The result was a willing little car admirably suited to hilly country. It was capable of over 50 mph (80 km/h), not to mention 30 (50 km/h) in second. These characteristics were nearly the 509's undoing, for the engine ran fast, and the oil pump could not always cope,

The laurel wreath in the badge used by Fiat in the 1920s commemorated their success in racing.

1927 Fiat 509A

When a separate chassis is used there is no limit to possible body styles, and there were at least six 509A Fiat variants current in 1927. For commercial users there were also a light van and the torpedo commerciale, *illustrated here. This had a detachable rear seat and tailgate, making it a truck for weekdays and a family tourer for weekends.*

The 509 of 1925, Fiat's first cheap small car to see volume production, received enormous publicity, with special factory-backed insurance and hire-purchase schemes. This poster is typical of the promotion campaign.

especially with a two-bearing crankshaft. Once the amateur tuners laid hands on the model (inevitable in Italy!) the failings became plain. Without any publicity, the oiling arrangements were revised in the summer of 1926, and the 509A, illustrated left, resulted. (The two engines can easily be distinguished: on later ones the carburetter is on the left rather than on the right side).

With these improvements the Fiat became more reliable and evolved into a best-seller. Total production was over 90,000 cars, and it is significant that the model's last year – 1929 – was also commercially its best, with over 24,000 units delivered.

Though the full-house sports variants – as much as 36 bhp were extracted from a low-chassis supercharged edition, the *Sport Monza* – were made only in small numbers, a whole variety of standard coachwork was available – roadsters, tourers, two- and four-seater coupés, cabriolets, sedans in several styles, and delivery types such as a *torpedo commerciale* (tourer with tailgate and detachable rear seating) and a van. The Fiat's generous 100-inch (2·55 m) wheelbase permitted four-door bodies as yet found on only one other cheap baby, Singer's Junior, which was largely a British home-market item anyway. Among the specialist coachbuilders to work on the 509A chassis was William Lyons's Swallow firm, who fitted some late models with variations on the curvaceous two-door sports saloon theme already seen on the Austin Seven.

Franklin 11-B

1927, United States

Air cooling had few adherents in the 1920s, and almost all of these made light cars with motor-cycle-type engines. An exception was the Franklin from upstate New York, where it had been made–always with this type of power unit–since 1902.

Herbert Franklin's credo of 'scientific light weight' went further than dispensing with a radiator and its attendant plumbing. Light alloy was liberally utilized: the firm had been a pioneer of the aluminium piston and had even tried aluminium fenders before 1920. Suspension was by full-elliptic springs all round, while the light but robust frames were of ash, not pressed steel.

The 1927 car illustrated has, of course, a conventional appearance, but only because the firm's Los Angeles distributor had protested against the hideous 'horsecollar' bonnet used between 1922 and 1924. Frank de Causse's new and elegant idiom would grace the 1925–29 models, and be imitated by such watercooled machinery as Chandler and Durant.

By upper middle-class American standards, the car's six-cylinder overhead-valve engine was undersized and underpowered–only 32 bhp claimed from 3·3 litres. Wheelbase was 119 inches (3·02 m), but low weight permitted the 60 mph (100 km/h) norm expected from this type of vehicle. Cooling was by a frontal sirocco fan, and like most American makers, Franklin used a three-speed unit gearbox, dry-plate clutch, and vacuum feed. Oddly, though, they would not adopt four-wheel brakes (of hydraulic type) until 1928. In 1927 the pedal still actuated a drum on the transmission.

Considering the vehicle's heterodoxy and relatively high price, sales were good, and would build up to a peak of 14,000 in 1929. Understanding, the flying fraternity were Franklin-oriented: Charles A. Lindbergh, Donald Douglas and Amelia Earhart all drove this make.

The Franklin lion mascot used from 1925 to 1928.

1927 Franklin 11-B

1927 Itala 61

Itala's 1928 sports car was created by lowering the Tipo 61 chassis and adding a twin-overhead camshaft head. The ingenious means of passing the rear axle through the frame members is shown here.

Itala 61

1927, Italy

In 1927 Italy still made luxury motor-cars for affluent Europeans. The Itala company might be nearly bankrupt after a disastrous wartime foray into aero-engine manufacture, but they never compromised the standards that had bred Grand Prix racers, the winner of the Peking-Paris race, and transport for the House of Savoy before 1914.

They had, however stepped down from 7-litre giants to a variation on the 2-litre high-performance theme also favoured by Delage (pages 38–9) and Sizaire Frères (page 37). A straightforward pressed-steel chasis, four-wheel brakes, wire wheels and balloon tyres were the accepted norm, but Itala's anchors had servo assistance, and designer G. C. Cappa preferred a pushrod six for greater flexibility. This beautifully-made little unit had seven mains, pump cooling, and magneto ignition, while the three-speed box of prototypes gave way to a four-speeder on production models. Friction dampers were fitted, and the usual Rolls-Royce-shaped radiator gave the car the 'Italian look'. The result was quiet and smooth, but not very fast. Even a simple tourer weighed 2,772 lb (1,255 kg), and top speed was only in the low 60s (100–105 km/h). Bearing failures were not uncommon either.

Further, Itala's approach to a financial crisis was less than realistic. While the 61 was under development they were playing with a fantastic 1,100 cc racer with front-wheel drive, wooden frame, and V12 engine! This left no spare cash for the attractive 65 sports car, a 61 derivative with twin overhead-camshaft engine in a low chassis on which the rear axle passed through the frame side-members. This one should have attracted sportsmen, though curiously it was a 61 that took eighth place at Le Mans in 1928. Itala struggled on, always in receivership, until 1934.

La Salle 303

1927, United States

Officially the Cadillac-built La Salle 303 of 1927 marks the beginning of automobile styling. This is incorrect: Frank de Causse had given a facelift to Franklin (page 56) in 1925, preceded by work for Locomobile. The difference was that Harley Earl was hired by Lawrence Fisher of General Motors to inject some beauty into the Cadillac line, and given his own department in which to work.

How to make last year's model look different: the fine bonnet louvres on this 1929 La Salle are a great improvement on the coarser pattern found on the first cars.

The result was clearly inspired by the Franco-Spanish Hispano-Suiza (pages 16–17). It was also a better-looking car than the rival Packard. Packard led Cadillac in the sales stakes, and would continue so to do until 1932. And while other 'companion makes' within General Motors (Oakland's Pontiac, for instance) were cheap, cut-price offerings, the La Salle, though less expensive – prices started below \$3,000 (£600) – was also lighter, faster and handier than a Cadillac. A roadster averaged 95 mph (155 km/h) on test for 1,000 miles, and the standard article was good for over 80 (130 km/h). Wheelbase was 125 inches (3·17 m) to the Cadillac's 132 (3·378 m).

Mechanically, the car was a slightly scaled-down Cadillac with a smaller, 5-litre edition of the 90-degree side-valve V8, in unit with a three-speed gearbox and dry-plate clutch. The water pump was supplemented by thermostatically controlled radiator shutters, and there was an auxiliary mechanical petrol pump as well as the vacuum feed to cut out starvation on hills. The four-wheel brakes were of mechanical type.

Customers had a choice of nine bodies, plus a long-wheelbase option for seven-seaters. Custom styles by Fleetwood were also available, and nearly 11,000 La Salles sold in the first year. Along with Cadillac, the make would pioneer the clashproof synchromesh gearbox in 1929.

Léon Bollée 12CV

1927, France

International manufacturing networks were uncommon in the 1920s. General Motors, of course, controlled Vauxhall in England, and Ford had factories in Australia, Britain, France and Germany, but that was the limit. Thus W. R. Morris's attempts to invade the French industry from within were revolutionary. Opening his Paris showroom in 1924 had had no effect: the Morris-Cowley was not the sort of car the French wanted. Thus when opportunity arose to acquire the old Léon Bollée plant at Le Mans, Morris jumped smartly into the breach.

Léon himself had died in 1913, and his widow had carried on the business as best she could, turning out sound middle-class cars of dubious profitability in the 2/3-litre class. That Morris had higher ambitions was shown when he hired Rolls-Royce's former Paris service manager, and ordered 2,500 sets of components for his new 12CV challenger. Amusingly, its 2·4-litre overhead-valve four-cylinder engine came from Harry Ainsworth of Hotchkiss, whom Morris had fired when he took over that firm's Coventry works. This engine was also found in contemporary Hotchkisses.

What emerged from Le Mans might look like a Morris-Oxford with Bollée radiator, but it was a typical French family tourer with magneto ignition, four-speed gearbox, mechanical four-wheel brakes and half-elliptic springs. A dry-plate clutch was used instead of Morris's familiar wet-plate type, while both gearshift and steering were on the right-hand side. A reliable machine, it could cruise steadily at 50mph (80km/h). Sales averaged 2,500 a year for several seasons – good for such a machine, but not good enough for Morris.

By the end of the 1920s stylistic trends had crossed the Atlantic, and by 1932 the 12CV Léon Bollée had been given a ribbon-type radiator shell in Chrysler style.

The French resented the interloper, and disliked selling components to him. Thus, though Morris hung on to his Gallic empire until 1931, the 12CV's subsequent stablemates, thinly-disguised overhead-camshaft Wolseley sixes and straight-eights, met with no success at all.

After Morris sold out, the company lingered on for a while under independent English management. Morris-Bollée will, however, be chiefly remembered as the 'Bentley Boys'' depot during the triumphant years at Le Mans.

1927 Léon Bollée 12CV

Maximag

1927, Switzerland

Switzerland protected—and, on paper, still protects—her motor industry, but this has never amounted to much. Anti-motoring sentiments lingered here far longer than in almost any other country, and even in 1929 the Confederacy registered a mere 55,000 cars, with Fiat, Citroën and Ford as the best-sellers. Switzerland's most famous factory, Martini, probably turned out less than 2,000 units in 33 years.

The Maximag is less familiar. It lasted only from 1922 to 1928, and production was probably about 200 cars, to judge from 1931 returns, which show 140 still in use then. Its makers, Motosacoche of Geneva, were, however, almost a household word. Their first product had been a 'tool bag motor' (hence the name) or auxiliary clip-on engine for bicycles. Thence they had progressed to motor-cycles proper, ably supported by the MAG proprietary power unit, fitted to countless motorbikes and cyclecars from almost every part of Europe.

A publicity poster showing the open sports Maximag.

1927 Maximag

Already in 1914 they had shown an overhead-camshaft four-cylinder car engine giving 33 bhp from 1,100 cc though nothing so exciting went into their own vehicles. These used a simple side-valve of like capacity, rated at 20 bhp, cooled by thermo-siphon, and with magneto ignition. There were three forward speeds, the clutch was a multi-disc, and drive was transmitted to the spiral bevel rear axle. There was also semi-pressure lubrication. The car sold for the equivalent of £280 in its homeland. A few reached France, but the Maximag was not generally exported.

By 1927, there had been some improvements. Front-wheel brakes were available, as was a 30 bhp sports model with four forward speeds, capable of nearly 70 mph (110 km/h). This one had an overhead-valve engine and was listed until the end.

Minerva 12CV

1927, Belgium

Switzerland's motor industry never got off the ground. Belgium's, by contrast, had a long and distinguished career. Names like Excelsior, FN, Germain, Métallurgique, Nagant, Pipe and – especially – Minerva were world-renowned. Unfortunately, the FN apart, they were all large and expensive cars aimed primarily at rich Frenchmen, Germans and Britons. In the 1920s, relaxation of domestic tariffs let in first the American assembly plants at Antwerp and then France's cheaper models. By the time the Great Depression struck, nobody was buying Belgian any more, though Minerva's splendid sleeve-valve carriages survived into 1936.

Minerva had adopted the Silent Knight engine as keenly as had Daimler in England, though their offerings had never been so consistently directed at the dowager market – the 6-litre AKS of 1929 could give a comparable Bentley or Hispano-Suiza a good run for its money. Their main business had, however, been formal carriages. The 5·3-litre six of 1919 was followed by the AK, and ultimately by a 6·6-litre straight-eight.

This was fine while the customers were there: Minerva sold an impressive 2,500 units in 1925. But Sylvain de Jong, the company's head, saw the need for something smaller and cheaper. The 2-litre 12CV took its bow at the 1926 shows.

As always, the engine was a Knight. In deference to prevailing fashions it was a six, on modern lines with coil ignition and vacuum feed. With an eye to its American rivals, it used a three-speed gearbox and central change, while brakes (on all four wheels, of course) had vacuum-servo assistance. Minerva's traditional pump-and-trough lubrication was retained, but bodies were fabric. Minerva hoped to drum up business by charging the same price for tourers and saloons, but though very quiet, *la fille de Minerva* (Minerva's daughter, as press releases called her) was heavy – 3,409 lb (1,540 kg) and thirsty. Sleeve-valve engines might not need decarbonizing, but they were expensive to make and to repair. Though the model was still quoted in 1933, it did not bring the hoped-for salvation.

An earlier and bigger six-cylinder sleeve-valve Minerva engine dating from 1920–21 and remarkably neat in appearance. Worth noting are the vacuum tank for the fuel feed in the firewall and the elaborate inlet manifold.

Minerva's goddess mascot.

Talbot 14/45 hp

1927, Great Britain

Georges Roesch, Clement Talbot's Swiss chief engineer, set out to produce a Twenty Rolls-Royce in miniature—half the size, half the weight, and half the price. He did even better: the end-product sold for £395 ($1,975) or about a quarter of the sum asked for a Rolls with fairly simple bodywork.

The design was versatile. What started with 1·7 litres and 41 bhp had evolved in a decade into cars of up to 3·4 litres and 123 bhp, and competition versions achieved a lot more than this. In addition, the engine had been married to the best of the early semi-automatic boxes, Roesch's 'accelerating pre-selector', on which no manual effort was required for upward shifts. The 14/45's successors managed a third and a fourth at Le Mans in 1930, as well as distinguishing themselves in TT races and Alpine Trials. The design also formed the basis of London's standard ambulance; many such Talbots served right through the 1939–43 Blitz.

All this spelt prosperity for Talbot. But what Roesch had inherited was a run-down and bankrupt factory, so he had to take the gamble of ordering the 14/45 into production straight off the drawing-board. The risk came off. Over 11,000 of this smallest Talbot would be sold in nine seasons, no mean feat with a middle-class car in the teeth of a worldwide slump.

Detail design was ingenious. The frame was rigidly cross-braced, the radiator was mounted directly on the crankcase, steering joints were permanently lubricated, and the engine oil was used—under pressure, of course—to lubricate the four-speed gearbox as well. Starting was by a silent dynamotor driven off the nose of the four-bearing crankshaft (bigger Talbots had seven mains). The six-cylinder unit featured ultra-light overhead-valve gear, bi-metal pistons, 12-volt coil ignition, and vacuum feed. The traditional right-hand gearshift was retained, brakes were rod-operated on all four wheels, and rear springs were quarter-elliptic. A long 120-inch (3,048-m) wheelbase meant plenty of body shape. Other unusual details were the warning light instead of an oil pressure gauge, and the arrow-type turn signals built into the rear number plate. Roesch gave all his new designs intensive workouts in his native Switzerland.

Though bigger sports Talbots, such as the 2·3-litre 90, were available from 1930 onward, the basic 14 hp soldiered on, now renamed the 65 (its designed maximum speed in mph). Wire instead of artillery wheels were used from 1930, a silent third gearbox came in 1932, and preselection in 1933. A wide range of bodies—including some 'approved' customs—was always offered. In 1928/9 the 14/45 could be had as roadster, touring, fabric and coachbuilt two-seater coupés and four-door saloons, a fabric sportsman's coupé with rear trunk, and a formal limousine with division. None cost more than £550 ($2,750).

◄*Two generations of sports-racing car in the Double-Twelve at Brooklands in 1930. On the left are Lewis and Eaton with a 2·3-litre Talbot 90 and, on the right, Clement and Watney's 6·6-litre Bentley. Direct descendants of the original 14/45, the racing Talbots remained suitable for road use and went about their work in uncanny silence.*

►*A typical piece of 1929 styling: the Sportsman's Coupé, with its blind rear quarters, a large but not very practical trunk at the rear, and fabric-covered body. Talbot's version had a sliding roof as well, while the fully opening windscreen was a boon in fog.*

But nothing is perfect: the price paid for first-class brakes, handling and suspension was mechanical complexity. The big dynamotor used a lot of current, calling for 24-volt systems on the larger Talbot engines. In old age, Roesch's cars became mechanics' nightmares: they had been designed to go long distances between major services, but these services were the preserve of specialists.

Moreover, after 1937 there was no factory dealer network. The profitable Talbot operation in Kensington had always been bedevilled by its two associate (and money-losing) companies, Sunbeam of Wolverhampton and Darracq in Paris, and the combine collapsed as Roesch's cars approached their zenith. The Rootes brothers came to the rescue, but their idea of a rescue lay in attaching the Talbot badge (plus the radiator and some of the elegance) to Hillmans and Humbers, complete with side-valve engines. There were 1938 Talbots (and Sunbeam-Talbots for many years thereafter), but these owed nothing whatever to Georges Roesch.

1927 Talbot 14/45 hp

Volvo ÖV4/PV4

1927, Sweden

Today, Volvo are big business: 171,000 cars made in 1977, a branch factory in Holland and a powerful stake in the world's heavy truck markets. But when Assar Gabrielsson and Gustav Larson planned their Swedish 'national car' in 1927, they were dependent not only on outside backing but on outside component suppliers. (Penta, who made their engines, are now a Volvo subsidiary.) They were also content with modest sales: production would not break 2,000 a year until 1939.

The idiom chosen was that of a compact American type, design being partly the work of Ivan Ornberg from Hupmobile. Simplicity and a good ground clearance for bad roads were the keynotes. The engine was a three-bearing side-valve four of 1·9 litres capacity, pressure-lubricated, but with coil ignition. There were three forward speeds, wheels were wood artillery, and bodies wood-framed, though, unusually, brakes worked only on the rear wheels. A modified version of the chassis was used for light trucks.

1927 Volvo ÖV4/PV4

The Volvo in fabric saloon form.

The car was nearly a flop, but only because Sweden's arctic climate had been ignored and a tourer body standardized. A fabric saloon was hurriedly added, and Volvo's 'Jakob' went on to sell 996 units in two years.

Willys-Knight 66A

1927, United States

Licences to build the Knight sleeve-valve engine were restricted. American licencee John N. Willys, predictably, made more such units than anyone else. In 1928, the make's banner year, 55,000 of his middle-class Willys-Knights found buyers. These, of course, complemented the cheap Whippet (formerly Overland). They were Buick and Chrysler competitors; alongside the big 3·9-litre 66 on its 126-inch (3·2-m) wheelbase was a less expensive 3-litre 70. The high cost of manufacture was, however, reflected in the $1,495 (£300) asked even for this.

Its engine apart, the big Willys-Knight reflected the contemporary American idiom. In this class, seven-bearing crankshafts and full-pressure lubrication were commonplace, while an output of 65 bhp gave an adequate if unspectacular performance. The four-wheel brakes were of the usual expanding-and-contracting type, electrics were 6-volt, and the carburetter was vacuum-fed. The car had quite a distinguished appearance, with its horizontal bonnet louvres and stylized, shield-shaped headlamp shells. From 1927 a long (135-in/3·42-m) chassis was offered for seven-seater bodies, though for Knight fans in quest of real luxury, Stearns, a Willys subsidiary, offered their magnificent straight-eight.

Like other Willys products, the 66 was assembled in Britain in the Willys-Overland-Crossley plant at Stockport. The 1929 models (66B) were styled by Amos Northup, and were far more elegant, especially the 'plaidside' sports roadsters.

Willys's Knight mascot of 1927, a pun on the company's Knight sleeve-valve engine. Early mascots have no lance.

Clyno 9

1928, Great Britain

Clyno of Wolverhampton sought to challenge Morris on insufficient capital. Thus their life was short, if merry–seven seasons and 36,000 cars. The firm's name had been made with the 1·4-litre Eleven, a Morris-Cowley competitor. Morris, however, were known to be planning a baby car, and Clyno were determined to get in first. They did–by nine months.

Engineering was simple–a 950cc side-valve four with magneto ignition, pump-and-trough lubrication, thermo-siphon cooling, and gravity feed. There was a three-speed unit gearbox with central change, the frame had three cross-members, and rear springs were quarter-elliptic, though even on so utilitarian a car, four-wheel brakes were now mandatory. Fabric bodies cut both cost and drumming. Price of a saloon was £160: it weighed 1,244 lb (563 kg), attained 50 mph (80 km/h), and returned 40–45 mpg (6·3–7 lit/100).

But rumour now spoke of a £100 Morris, and Clyno panicked. Specifications were pared further (no plated brightwork, a three-lamp lighting set) for the Century tourer, still short of the magic figure at £112·50. Quality suffered–and the trade's nickname ('Cemetery') proved a true bill. Clyno died in May, 1929.

1928 Clyno 9

Daimler Double-Six-30

1928, Great Britain

As yet, the ultimate in smoothness and silence meant more cylinders, as Packard and their fellow-Americans had discovered in 1915. Europe's first commercially-produced 12 was the English sleeve-valve Daimler, designed by Laurence Pomeroy and unveiled at the 1926 London Show.

The first cars were 7·1-litre giants. The engine was essentially a pair of 25 hp bi-block Daimler-Knight sixes on a common crankcase: it well merited its name of Double-Six for there were two of everything per block – magneto and coil ignitions, carburetters, and water pumps. Sleeves were now steel instead of cast iron as on earlier Daimlers; the seven-bearing crankshaft incorporated a vibration damper; and lubrication was of full-pressure type. Pistons and crankcase were of aluminium, other features including a four-speed gearbox with central change, an underslung worm back axle, and vacuum-servo four-wheel brakes with a transmission handbrake.

The car would accelerate silently from a standstill to its 82 mph (131 km/h) maximum in top, but the result was elephantine, especially with the optional 163-inch (4·13 m) wheelbase. Weight was over three tons, and fuel was consumed at the rate of a gallon every eight miles (35 lit/100). Though a sports saloon was catalogued, this was not really a car for the owner-driver.

In 1928, therefore, came the scaled-down 30 of 3·7-litres' capacity, and with only one set of plugs per cylinder. The car had, however, the same complex steering gear (to clear the wide engine). It was still quite a lot of car, too, weighing around two tons, and with 102 inches (nearly 2·6 m) of *body* space available with the longest wheelbase option. The 16 mpg (17·5 lit/100) consumption was more realistic, too. Daimler 30s were good for 70–75 mph (112–120 km/h) and were supplied both to King George V and also to Queen Mary.

▼ *A central bar on the radiator identifies 12-cylinder Daimlers, but swivelling headlamps were a special extra.*

►*Front view of the complicated Daimler Double Six sleeve-valve engine made from 1927 to 1935.*

▲ *1930 Model-As on a transporter using a Ford AA tractive unit.*

Ford Model-A

1928, United States

In May, 1927, the last of some 16 million Model-T 'Tin Lizzies' rolled off the Ford lines; its successor followed seven months later. That Henry Ford had once again picked the right formula was shown by sales of more than five million in just over four years. But the formula's relatively short life – in relation to 'Lizzie's 18-year span – also suggested a more critical public.

Inherited from olden days were a splash-lubricated four-cylinder engine, a compact 106-inch (2·69-m) wheelbase, gravity feed, and the tough all-transverse suspension. The new Ford, however, had some of the elegance of its prestige stablemate, the Lincoln (page 46); it also had a conventional three-speed box with central change, and the four-wheel brakes now virtually universal. It was, admittedly, not one of the world's best stoppers, but the gearchange was likened to 'running a knife through melted butter', and it had the T's dependability without 'Lizzie's idiosyncrasies. With 3·3 litres and 40 bhp, the car was capable of 60–65 mph (100–105 km/h), and it sold for under $500 (£100) at home. For tax-conscious export markets (Britain, France) a small-bore 2-litre edition (Model-AF) was offered.

Model-As were built in Ford's foreign plants from England to Australia. Commercial versions for payloads of up to $1\frac{1}{2}$ tons paralleled the private cars, and the range of bodies extended from the smart roadster (worth a fortune in the collector-market of the 1980s) to America's first volume-produced woody station wagon. The A would also form the cornerstone of the Soviet Union's automobile industry, taking countless car, truck and military guises in Russia. The commercial GAZ-AA was still being manufactured there as late as 1948. Though Chevrolet had edged ahead during Model-T's decline, Ford would resume the sales lead in 1929 and 1930, delivering over a million units in each year.

Imperia 10CV

1928, Belgium

Belgian Imperias of the 1920s used slide valves recessed into the cylinder walls. These were opened and closed by double cams without the use of springs. These engines worked well, but were expensive to overhaul.

Unlike most Belgian cars, the Imperia was quite small–even the six-cylinder car illustrated ran to only 1·6 litres–and reasonably priced: £475 in England. Heterodoxy extended beyond the top end: the 10CV's companion four cranked anti-clockwise, and on all pre-1932 models the brakes were uncoupled. The pedal worked (with considerable ferocity) on front wheels and transmission, leaving the lever to cope with the rear wheels. The monobloc engine was pressure-lubricated and gravity-fed, with thermo-siphon cooling and coil ignition. The four-speed gearbox was of unit type.

Imperia made a serious bid to keep the national industry alive, and by 1929 they had built up a small empire embracing Excelsior (now building 10CV bodies), Métallurgique, and the coachbuilders Matthys & Osy. They also negotiated an agreement with Voisin in France (from which little resulted) and there were even plans to assemble Imperias in Britain in the old GWK works at Maidenhead.

Despite the Depression, production had been worked up to 725 cars (233 of them sixes) in 1930, but thereafter sales fell away and in 1934 Imperia turned to the licence-manufacture of German Adlers.

Maybach W5SG

1928, Germany

The cars of Karl Maybach, son of the original Mercedes designer, were always large, expensive and complex. The smallest engine used was a $3\frac{1}{2}$-litre; weights exceeded two tons; and from 1930 the flagship of the range was an 8-litre V12. About 2,000 were produced between 1921 and 1940.

The W5 illustrated was their largest six, a 7-litre affair with horizontal overhead valves and twin camshafts. Head and pistons were of light alloy, there was dual ignition, and mechanical pump fuel feed. Brakes were servo-assisted hydro-mechanical, but the principal interest centred round the transmission arrangements.

The Maybach's simple lines give no clue to its mechanical complexity. The belt moulding in contrasting colour shows American influence, and the twin wipers traverse instead of moving in an arc as on modern cars.

Initially, Maybach had used a simple, pedal-controlled two-speed box on Model-T Ford lines, admittedly with servo-assistance. Oddly though, the more powerful the engine, the more complex were the means used to deliver the power to the back axle. On 1928 editions of the W5, there was a two-speed overdrive unit behind the main box, with selection by a right-hand lever, though it could also be engaged by flooring the accelerator. This gave a high range, reducing engine speed at 50 mph (80 km/h) from 2,400 to 1,500 rpm. The Maybach overdrive, or *schnellgang*, was commercially marketed, and available on several German luxury makes of the period. The last W5s – and subsequent Maybach models – had the even more complex *doppelschnellgang*: eight forward speeds and four reverses!

Packard's Goddess of Speed mascot, 1928.

Packard's badge bears the family coat-of-arms.

Packard Eight
1928, United States

In an era increasingly dominated by the stylist, Packards stayed ageless. Two concessions to the march of time were made between 1923 and 1939: a vee-radiator for 1932, and a vee-windshield to match it six years later. Packard offered factory-backed used cars long before the idea was taken up by the Big Battalions. On most – if not all – models badging was confined to the hubcaps. In the 1920s, every Packard was a quality product, and most of them were straight-eights: the old Twin Six had faded out in 1923, and 1928 would be the Single Six's last season. New developments were subjected to long-distance trials on Packard's proving-grounds.

What one got for one's money – $3,500 (£700) in America – was a nine-bearing side-valver on orthodox American lines, coil ignition, vacuum feed, three-speed unit gearbox, semi-elliptic springs, and the mechanical four-wheel brakes standardized back in 1923. From 1927, a hypoid bevel rear axle (not general practice in Europe till the 1950s) had been adopted to lower the body line. Packard's disc wheels were of full-demountable type; all 1928's eights shared the same 6·3-litre engine and 143-inch (3·63 m) wheelbase; and top speed was a quiet 80 mph (128 km/h). Over 50,000 Packards found buyers in 1928.

The company listed its cars by series rather than by model year, though the fifth series run coincided with the 1928 season. It took a practised eye to tell one series from another, the main visible difference between 1928s and 1927s being the new moulded-rubber steering-wheel rim.

Röhr R-Type

1928, Germany

Straight-eights were in fashion by 1928: smoothness and a longer bonnet outweighed the nuisance of 'two more of everything' to maintain. At peak, ten German makers had such a type in their catalogues, though few of them could compete against American imports.

The Röhr was, however, no mock-American. It used an overhead-valve engine, whereas almost all Detroit's eights were side-valvers. Capacity was only 2 litres, soon increased to 2·2. The car was relatively small,

1928 Röhr R-Type.

weighing in at 2,275 lb (1,030 kg), and priced to compete with Mercedes-Benz's stolid 'Stuttgart' six. More important still, it used H. G. Röhr's own all-independent suspension, by double transverse springs at the front, and by swing axles at the rear. Ride, handling and brakes were all excellent, though, on a modest 50 bhp, performance was unspectacular. For the rest, Röhr's eights ran to nine main bearings, featured pressure lubrication and coil ignition, and transmitted their power via a three-speed gearbox and dry multi-plate clutch to a worm-drive back axle. Brakes were mechanical, though hydraulics, along with synchromesh gears and a free wheel, featured from 1930 on.

The factory was said to be building four cars a day in mid-1928, and hoped soon to be making ten. Only about 1,300 were, however, delivered in the first three seasons, and after Röhr left to join Adler in 1932, the venture's days were numbered.

Voisin 14CV

1928, France

Gabriel Voisin was one of France's most idiosyncratic designers, with strong views on everything. He always insisted on adequate luggage accommodation, hence the large boxes found on the running-boards of factory-bodied cars. He was also addicted to the Knight double-sleeve-valve engine, extracting more urge (and revs) from it than most other users. He detested rumble-seat roadsters and chromium plate, and mistrusted hydraulic brakes. Mechanicals with vacuum-servo assistance were found on the little 2·3-litre six offered

Voisin's winged badge.

from late 1926 and illustrated opposite.

Voisin had tested this engine in an unsuccessful streamlined Grand Prix car back in 1923; hence the production model's respectable 56 bhp – developed incidentally at a 4,400 rpm which automatically invalidated the guarantee if an owner explored it (3,500 rpm was Voisin's prescribed engine speed)! Pressure lubrication, vacuum feed, and silent dynamotor starting were among the features, while Voisin was another recent recruit to coil ignition. The semi-elliptic springs were reinforced by hydraulic dampers. A three-speed gearbox was standard; it could be supplemented by a two-speed rear axle, range-selection being by a right-hand floor lever. In high range the 14CV cruised at 65–70 mph (108–112 km/h). This was good for a 3,000 lb (1,360 kg) sedan. Interestingly, factory-bodied convertibles already had crash hoops in their tops.

The model remained in Voisin catalogues until the mid-30s, about 8,000 being made. In 1934, the factory was offering works-reconditioned 14CVs for about a quarter of the then new price.

Brennabor AS
1929, Germany

By 1928, Germany's motor industry had made up much of the lost leeway. Brennabor of Brandenburg, now forgotten, was one of the country's major factories, with 6,000 hands and a production which jumped from 100 a month in 1923 to 100 a day with the installation of a moving assembly line (already adopted by Opel).

The A-type six introduced in 1927 could have been mistaken for an American Oakland, and the formula was American: side valves, pump cooling, 6-volt coil ignition, vacuum feed, central change and mechanical four-wheel brakes. The four-speed box of the first cars had given way to a three-speeder on the 3·1-litre version illustrated, and long chassis variants even wore wood wheels. Performance was average: 55–60 mph (90–100 km/h) with a 19 mpg (15 lit/100) thirst.

Brennabors were often seen with that typically German style, the cabrio-limousine, or full sedan with folding top. Competitive pricing at the equivalent of £300–325 ensured brisk sales (10,000 units) for the A family, though the smaller Juwel, its replacement, fared less well, and a straight-eight derivative was hardly ever seen. The last Brennabors were delivered in 1934.

1929 Brennabor AS

Voisin's stylized eagle mascot.

1928 Voisin 14CV

Chevrolet International Six

1929, United States

Chevrolet has long been known as the world's best-selling automobile, and the famous 'Cast Iron Wonder' was the car that put the make firmly (if not immediately) in the lead. Since then, even Ford's most determined endeavours have never dislodged the 'Chevy' for long.

In one respect, of course, the Chevrolet had the edge on both the Ford and on Chrysler's new cut-price Plymouth: it was a six, whereas the opposition stayed with fours. (The Ford V8 would be a 1932 debutante and the PC Plymouth arrived a year later.) In other respects – the overhead valves apart – the

1929 Chevrolet International Six

car followed the Great American Norm.

Three main bearings and splash lubrication were adequate on an engine intended to do its work at a gentle 2,600 rpm, though Chevrolet preferred a mechanical pump to Ford's gravity fuel feed or Plymouth's vacuum arrangements. Curiously, though, the petrol gauge on 1929 cars stayed out of doors, on the tank. The plate clutch, three-speed gearbox, and torque tube drive were regular Chevrolet practice, as were the expanding-and-contracting mechanical four-wheel brakes: at the cheap end of the market, only Plymouth offered hydraulics. The chromium-plated brightwork was a sign of the times, but while wheels were steel discs, they were still of fixed type with demountable rims: Ford alone used standardized, full-detachable equipment.

Wheelbase, at 107 inches (2.72 m), was between Ford's and Plymouth's; Chevrolet had already added the extra length on 1928's last fours, in anticipation of the American industry's subsequent practice of alternating chassis/body and mechanical changes between years. Springs were, of course, semi-elliptic. The engine gave an average 46 bhp from 3·2 litres, and the four-door sedan's weight of 2,585 lb (1,170 kg) was higher than either of its four-cylinder rivals. Top speed, at 60/65 mph (100–105 km/h) was normal for this class of car.

The 1929 Chevrolet Six came in eight body styles, from a roadster at $525 (£105) to the seldom-seen landau sedan with drop back at $725 – still only the equivalent of about £145, and a lot less than Britons paid for the regular four-door model. In addition, there were light vans on the car chassis, and the LQ-series $1\frac{1}{2}$-ton truck to challenge Ford's AA. In this sector of the market, however, Chevrolet would not overtake Ford until 1933.

'The Six for the Price of a Four' was a natural winner: even in the darkest year of all, 1932, sales held above the 300,000 level. Early models might be short on looks and performance alike, but the simple engine lent itself to flat-rate servicing, hence a long run which did not end until 1953. To the end, it had only semi-pressure lubrication, but though capacity had been but slightly increased, to $3\frac{1}{2}$-litres, output was now an impressive 92 bhp.

The Chevrolet's subsequent evolution may be regarded as a commentary on American cheap-car design – all-expanding brakes in 1930, synchromesh in 1932, independent front suspension on 1934 models, hydraulic brakes in 1936, and true all-metal coachwork (plus hypoid rear axles) on the 1937 line. Britain was, curiously, one of the few markets of the 1930s where the Chevrolet Six made little impression. Truck versions, however, went into production in 1929 at Vauxhall's Luton works, giving way by 1931/2 to the closely related Bedford range.

The optional extra Chevrolet Viking mascot, 1929–31.

►*The most expensive 1929 Chevrolet, the landau sedan. Wood wheels were seldom fitted.*

◄*Chevrolet's 1929 tourer, a style then declining in popularity. The whitewall tyres are a later addition.*

Deguingand

1929, France

Even in France, its spiritual home, the cyclecar was virtually dead. Marcel Violet had, however, sponsored four breeds (Violet-Bogey, Sicam, Major and Sima-Violet) since constructing his first prototype in 1908, and was still at it. All these cars had used two-stroke engines; so did the Deguingand, made in the old Vinot factory.

It looked a real car with its sporty cycle fenders and pretty coupé or two-seater bodies. The engine was a vertical, watercooled four of 736 cc, with detachable head and dynamotor starting. Two speeds only were provided, while clutch and gearbox were mounted in unit with the differential back axle. A strange archaism was the use of a separate lever for reverse. Suspension was on Peugeot or Baby Austin lines–transverse at the front with quarter-elliptics at the rear–though four-wheel brakes were included. The tubular propeller shaft doubled as frame backbone.

The car was slow and very noisy. There was, incredibly, a proposal for British production in that graveyard of lost causes, Cordwalles Works, Maidenhead, but the Deguingand lasted only two seasons. Undeterred, Violet pursued the same theme on his Galba (1929) and Huascar (1931), the latter being subsequently marketed as the 4CV by Donnet of Nanterre.

1929 Deguingand

Horch 375

1929, Germany

Few firms were as dedicated to eight cylinders as Horch of Zwickau. From 1927 to 1939 they marketed a vast range of luxury straight-eights, joined in 1933 by a cheaper V8.

Vintage examples used a twin overhead-camshaft, five-bearing Paul Daimler design of engine, made for Horch by Argus of Berlin. This sophisticated unit was worked up from 3·1 litres and 60 bhp to 4 litres and 80 bhp. Pump cooling and coil ignition were used, and the machinery lived in an orthodox frame with four-speed gearbox, vacuum-servo brakes, and wood wheels. Left-hand steering was standard, but the centralized chassis lubrication was an unexpected refinement. The Horch 8 was, however, expensive, heavy and undistinguished in performance, with a well-substantiated reputation for running hot. It was, nevertheless, the first German eight-in-line to be made in significant numbers: nearly 7,000 of the twin-cam cars were sold in four seasons.

By 1929 some La Salle (page 58) influence was apparent in the styling, notably in the radiator with its thermostatic shutters. Frames were X-braced, and hydraulic dampers replaced the friction type, though hydraulic braking would not be added until the advent of Fritz Fiedler's much-improved single overhead-camshaft range in 1931.

The Horch badge.

Isotta Fraschini 8A

1929, Italy

Unkind critics dismiss the straight-eight Isotta Fraschini as the perpetual 'bridesmaid' among European super-cars of the 1920s, the 'bride', of course, being the Hispano-Suiza. This is a trifle harsh: the Isotta, after all, transported both Pope and King in its homeland, and it was always intended for chauffeur drive rather than for the enthusiastic owner. Further, in Italy's precarious economic climate, it relied on export sales for survival.

The company had been pioneers of front-wheel braking in 1909, and for their post-war eight, unveiled in 1919 (and thus a pioneer of this configuration), they used the coupled type; a necessary servo had been added on the later 8A announced in 1925. The engine had overhead valves, nine main bearings, and dual ignition, and gave 135 bhp. Like Hispano-Suiza, Isotta Fraschini considered three forward speeds quite enough, though unlike their Franco-Spanish rivals they preferred the American-style central change.

The massive frame had a wheelbase of 145 inches (3·7 m) and, even without bodywork, weight was 1,480 kg (3,272 lb). Bodies were to the client's whim, principal suppliers being Castagna and Sala. Prices of complete cars started at around £2,500 in England; in the United States, where a goodly proportion of the 950 8As were sold, one paid anything from $19,000 up.

Against a heavy and slip-prone clutch, heavy steering, some roughness at high speeds, and poor oil consumption had to be set looks, workmanship to match, durability, and a modest thirst for fuel – around 17 mpg (16–17 lit/100). Ford tried to buy Isotta in 1930, but the Italian Government blocked the sale, while Fascist rearmament would soon guide the firm into the safer realms of heavy trucks and aero engines. Very few cars were made after 1931.

1929 Horch 375

Morgan

1929, Great Britain

In Britain, there was still a market for sporting three-wheelers, reinforced by tax concessions. The law also permitted 16-year-olds to conduct 'non-reversible tricycles', though one had to be 17 to drive a proper car.

The Vintage Morgan might not be anyone's idea of a tricycle, but it was still innocent of reverse. Indeed, it was very like the first of the line, launched at the 1910 Motor-cycle Show – a tubular frame with central backbone and sliding-pillar independent front suspension. The single rear wheel was supported by a quarter-elliptic spring, and the driveline led from a vee-twin motor-cycle-type engine via a cone clutch to a two-speed bevel box, and thence by roller chain. Both brakes worked on the driving wheel. On sports Morgans the engine lived out of doors, though on softer species a simple cowl concealed the works. Standard wear on tourers was the side-valve JAP, either air- or watercooled.

For only £92 in 1929, one expected little refinement. True, electric lighting had been standardized since 1926, and all wheels were now braked; a coupled arrangement was not, however, offered and never would be on any twin-cylinder Morgan. There was no foot accelerator, the sight-feed oiling was authentic 1910, and the motor cranked from the side. As compensation, the motor could be withdrawn from the frame by undoing four bolts! The list price included a hood and three lamps, but speedometer and side curtains were extra, as were water cooling and a rather ineffectual electric starter.

Even the earliest Morgans could be had with Family bodies. This one is a 1912.

Variations on the touring Morgan theme included a 'family' model with room for two children, one each side of the back wheel, and a 'commercial' on which the rear seats were replaced by a box-carrier. For those who preferred a livelier and more Spartan 50 mph (80 km/h), the Morgan was an attractive buy. It was also a popular one; in the boom years Morgan's annual production ran at around 2,500 units.

Three Opels in a concours d'élégance. *The detachable wheels apart, styling is 1926 American.*

Opel 4/20 PS

1929, Germany

In the late 1920s the small European family car was settling down into a stereotyped mould. In the 1-litre class one expected a full four-seater capable of 50 mph (80 km/h), with four cylinders, four-wheel brakes, and semi-elliptic springs. The Opel represented the norm – apart from its quarter-elliptics at the rear.

These were understandable, for the 4/20 could trace its ancestry back to Germany's first assembly-line-built automobile, the 951 cc Laubfrosch (tree frog) of 1924. Apart from its green paintwork and an extra 95 cc of engine, this was a direct crib of the 5CV Citroën, even down to the suspension and the transmission footbrake. André Citroën may have been displeased, but Opel's sales jumped from 910 in 1923 to over 16,000 in 1925.

Next development was the 4/16 of 1927, still a two-bearing side-valve with gravity feed and thermo-siphon circulation, but now with half-elliptics at the front, brakes on all four wheels, a coil instead of the original magneto, and room for four. Capacity went up to 1,016 cc.

The 1929–30 models were much the same, apart from stiffer crankshafts and some more power – 20 instead of 16 bhp. Weight was around 1,600 lb (720 kg), and a roadster sold in Germany for the equivalent of £100, with £135 asked for a saloon. No wonder Opel's sales jumped to 34,578 in the last pre-Depression year, in which they were also taken over by General Motors. The make would soon account for 68 per cent of German car exports.

Renault Monasix

1929, France

The Renault losange *badge.*

An advertisement showing 1929's largest Renault, the straight-eight Reinastella, with frontal radiator.

Still under the autocratic direction of the founder, Renault in 1929 could be described as general providers. Their range of cars extended from the stolid 951 cc 6CV four up to the immense 7·1-litre eight-cylinder Reinastella, built by hand in small numbers. Other products included trucks of all sizes, buses for Paris and other cities, farm tractors, and aero engines, while a financial interest in Caudron had given them a stake in the light-plane industry as well.

With few exceptions, the product was stolid and uninspired, if also indestructible. Engines were the same old side-valves (now with monobloc cylinders) they had been for the last quarter of a century, still cooled by thermo-siphon, and still with coal-shovel bonnets and dashboard radiators. Although coil ignition was steadily ousting the magneto and cone clutches giving way to the single-plate type, the drive-line – a three-speed separately-mounted gearbox, torque tube, and spiral bevel back end – had gone unchanged throughout the 1920s. The mechanical brakes were none too effective, and the use of a

1929 Renault Monasix

transverse spring at the rear led to curious handling characteristics when there was performance enough to exploit them.

There seldom was. Lesser Renaults were built to churn down the *routes nationales* at 40–45 mph (60–70 km/h), and the tough and well-loved 2·1-litre KZ fours disposed of a mere 30 bhp. They were also noisy. The KZ would still be around in 1935, and when it departed, it would be replaced by an even bigger four.

Louis Renault was not, however, unaware of the growing fashion for 'Light Sixes', being quick off the mark with his own answer to Buick and Chrysler, the 3·2-litre Vivasix family. This was, however, too big to be used as a town runabout, a role filled for many years by the 6CV. Thus Renault's next step, in 1928, was a true pint-sized six for ladies, capable of doing all its work in top gear. It supplemented – and then supplanted – the ageing baby.

In its original form, the RY-type Monasix was copybook Renault, with side valves, dashboard radiator, and three forward speeds. There were 6-volt coil ignition and a single-plate clutch, and about 25 bhp were extracted from the four-bearing, 1,474 cc engine. Brakes were cable-operated, and flexibility was attained with the aid of low gearing: a 5·7 to 1 axle ratio on the first cars, dropping away to 6·5 as weights increased. The result was the ultimate in refined gutlessness: 60 mph (100 km/h) was claimed but 55 (90 km/h) was very hard work, though a gallon of petrol lasted 30 miles (9·4 lit/100). Unlike its later British counterparts (Wolseley Hornet, Triumph Scorpion) the Monasix was a full four-seater with four doors on a 111-inch (2·82 m) wheelbase.

By 1930 this model – and the rest of the Renault range – had acquired unit gearboxes and frontal radiators. Also offered was a *de-luxe* edition, the Monastella, with a wider range of bodies for about £40 more. The 1932 models no longer showed a vestige of the old coal-shovel styling; rather did they resemble foreshortened Chryslers. The advent of a new 7CV four that year heralded the end of the Monasix family, replaced at the close of the 1933 season by an 8CV of 1,463 cc. The car seems to have been reliable, as 11,000 were reported as still in usable condition in 1943.

Sima-Standard

1929, France

The 1929 Sima-Standard was an attempt to fill a gap at the bottom of the French market, left by Citroën's famous 5CV. This had been dropped in 1926. Of other French babies, both the 6CV Renault and Peugeot's Quadrilette family were obsolescent, leaving only one effective challenger in Lucien Rosengart's licence-built Austin Seven.

Further, Émile Dombret's new design used easily obtainable parts: the 856cc side-valve four-cylinder engine, chassis frame and quarter-elliptic rear springs were regular Citroën components. For the clutch, three-speed gearbox, and back axle, Dombret drew on Amilcar surplus, though proper four-wheel brakes replaced Citroën's transmission-and-rear-wheel arrangements, the front suspension was semi-elliptic, and on all but the first cars a coil replaced the magneto.

Styling was up to date, with the fashionable ribbon radiator shell. Saloons and tourers were full four-seaters: a van and a sporty roadster were also catalogued. Retention of Citroën's $92\frac{1}{2}$-inch (2·35 m) wheelbase assured compact dimensions, and the Sima was credited with 50 mph (80 km/h) and 43 mpg (6·5 lit/100). At 17,200 fr (£140), it was competitively priced.

A world depression was, however, no time to launch such a scissors-and-paste effort, and Sima died in 1932, though not before they had tried a companion 1·3-litre.

Singer Six

1929, Great Britain

By now, 2-litre British family cars tended to be sixes, though Hillman stayed with a four, and Austin offered both, their 12 and 16 sharing the same chassis and bodies. Singer, exceptionally, had been playing with small sixes as early as 1921: over the ensuing 16 years they would try side valves, pushrods and overhead camshafts, though nothing sold very well.

The 1929 cars derived from a smaller 1926

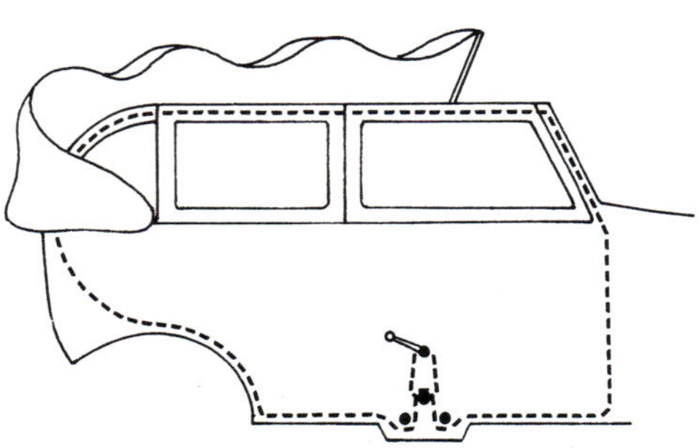

Saloon or tourer to order: Singer's version of the German cabrio-limousine with fixed sides and folding roof. The folding mechanism is remotely controlled by a handle on the driver's right.

1929 Singer Six

effort with three-bearing crankshaft and pump-and-trough lubrication. There was a unit-construction three-speed gearbox, fuel feed was by Autovac, and the four-wheel brakes soon acquired vacuum-servo assistance. Despite the twin carburetters, output was a staid 34 bhp.

Seven main bearings and pressure feed allowed 1929's 1·9-litre edition to run up to 4,000 rpm, and the quarter-elliptic springs of earlier days had given way to semi-elliptics all round. Advanced for the period were the hydraulic shock absorbers. The right-hand gate shift and central accelerator pedal reflected conservative British practice, and on a weight of 2,744 lb (1,260 kg) the Singer was no spectacular performer. Interestingly, though, the firm offered a convertible saloon with remotely controlled top, worked from the driver's seat.

Tatra T30

1929, Czechoslovakia

Bad roads (of which Czechoslovakia had more than her quota) make for sophisticated suspensions, and Hans Ledwinka's small Tatra featured all-independent arrangements from its inception in 1923. Transverse leaves were used at the front, with a swing axle at the rear – even on the first of his lightweights, 1,050 cc twins rated at 14 bhp, and without front-wheel brakes.

Nor did heresy stop here. The short, Renault-like snub nose swung up, complete with lamps and front wings, to reveal a horizontally-opposed, aircooled engine. This, with its four-speed unit gearbox, was built into a robust tubular backbone, with outriggers to carry the body. Ignition was by magneto, fuel was fed by gravity from a dash tank, and four-wheel brakes were standard from 1926.

In this year, the T11/12 twins were joined by the 1·7-litre T30 flat-four. On a modest 24 bhp it was a sedate performer, but the optional long wheelbase of 125 inches (3·17 m) made it suitable for taxi service.

The front-engined flat-four line would survive into 1948, bigger ones featuring one-shot chassis lubrication and hydraulic brakes. Latterly a conventionally-styled bonnet (still of one-piece, swing-up type) improved the looks, while six-wheeler developments of the T30 theme were widely used for cross-country and general military work.

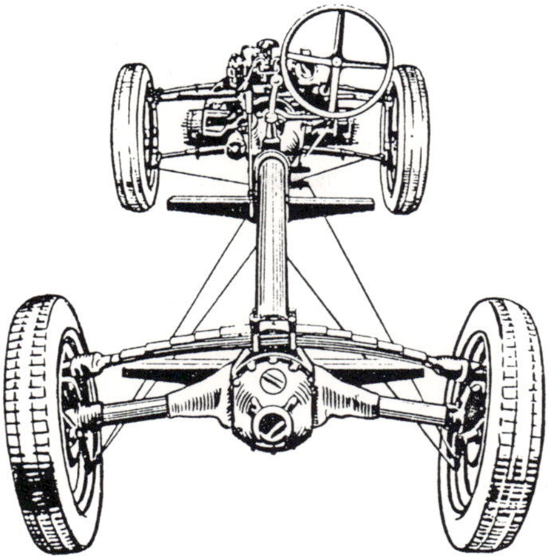

The Tatra's tubular backbone frame, all-independent springing, and body outriggers.

1929 Tatra T30

Cadillac 452

1930, United States

It is sometimes forgotten that a wave of economic optimism swept the world just before the Great Depression; hence the super-cars which furnished all the excitement at the 1930–31 shows.

While racing developments–notably 1926's 1,500cc Grand Prix Formula–had given the lie to the old contention that there was no substitute for litres, the quest for smoothness and silence had led to more and more cylinders. Automatic transmissions lay ten years in the future, so it was desirable to render shifting superfluous. Already, before World War I, there had been the V8s of de Dion-Bouton and Cadillac; Packard's V12 had been a wartime debutante; and in early Vintage times Duesenberg and Isotta Fraschini had put the straight-eight on the map. By 1929, the straight-eight was commonplace. In addition, although American industry had apparently dropped the 12, Europeans had a choice between the British Daimler, the German Maybach, and the French Voisin.

Soon the New World would again outstrip the Old. In 1932, deliveries of the best-selling Chevrolet might fall to barely 305,000, but affluent Americans had the choice of six native V12s and a brace of V16s. And of these last, Cadillac's was by far the more important.

One of three Cadillac mascots available in 1930: the Goddess.

The heraldic Cadillac badge.

Total sales of 4,386 16-cylinder automobiles in 11 seasons may sound unimpressive. What is more remarkable is that over three-quarters of these found buyers in the first two seasons–1930 and 1931–and this despite a price tag that would have bought ten Model-A Ford sedans. (With British import duty, the 16 cost as much as 20 Austin Sevens!) For this formidable outlay–and a 10mpg or 27 lit/100 thirst–one obtained the ultimate in smooth progression, a synchromesh gearbox as yet unobtainable on any European automobile, and a top speed in the region of 90mph (145km/h). Seven-seaters were rather slower: a roadster with the optional high-ratio rear axle was good for the magic 'ton' (160km/h).

Though no straight-eight car ever bore the Cadillac crest, the new model was a true double-eight with overhead valves and hy-

Later Cadillac V16s. On the 1933 (above) both wings and grille follow traditional lines, but on the 1934 (below) there are flowing lines, a forward-mounted engine and stylized 'biplane' bumpers

draulic valve lifters, developing 165 bhp. As on the earlier V12 Daimler (page 66), each bank of cylinders had its own carburetter, coil and manifolding, as well as its own vacuum feed. This arrangement was probably simpler in the long run, since a single component designed to cope with all 16 cylinders would have been a mechanic's nightmare. The gearbox was Cadillac's regular three-speed synchromesh, and the plate clutch a stronger edition of the V8's. The chassis rode on semi-elliptic springs, and the mechanical brakes, with drums of 16½-inch (41·9 cm) diameter, were given vacuum-servo assistance. Wheelbase was 148 inches (3·76 m), and a sedan weighed 5,850 lb (2,660 kg).

Equipment included a built-in radio aerial on closed cars, and 24 body styles – almost all handcrafted by General Motors' Fleetwood Body Division – were listed. Styling followed closely on that of Harley Earl's original La Salle (page 58), though by this time bonnet louvres had given way to doors.

A slightly less expensive V12 derivative was announced for 1931, and thereafter the 16 developed alongside the other Cadillac models. Clutches were servo-assisted from 1932, no-draught ventilation came in 1933, and X-braced frames with independent front suspension in 1934. The last of the old-type 16s were given hydraulic brakes in 1937, a year behind the rest of the range, and if some of the 'classic' looks were lost, the quality was not. By this time Cadillac felt confident enough to update the design, using a short-stroke side-valve engine for 1938. Alas for their hopes: America entered another recession, and the new 90 series expired in 1940 after a brief run.

Not, as one might imagine, a large overhead-camshaft four engine, but Lancia's narrow-angle 78, both neat and compact, and looking much smaller than its actual four litres.

De Soto CK
1930, United States

Youngest of America's Big Three, Walter P. Chrysler had attained comprehensive market coverage by 1930. While Plymouth took on Chevrolet and Ford, and the Chrysler line challenged Buick and La Salle, there were two middle-class offerings: the old-established Dodge and the all-new De Soto as a rival to Pontiac. Launched in 1928, the make had achieved a record for an all-new breed – 80,000 sold in the first year.

In effect only the name was new. The engineering was straightforward Chrysler, which meant all-expanding hydraulic brakes with a transmission handbrake. It also meant full-pressure lubrication for the six-cylinder side-valve engine, but in other respects the De Soto conformed to the regular American pattern: vacuum feed, three-speed gearbox, 6-volt electrics, and semi-elliptic springs. Wood wheels and demountable rims were standard; one paid extra for wire. Initially body styles bore Spanish names to commemorate the explorer Hernando de Soto, but by 1930 this gimmick had been dropped.

On the second-generation CK, illustrated below, there were few changes beyond a more powerful engine – 60 bhp from 3·1 litres. What had changed was the sales picture: down almost half from 1929's impressive level of 64,911 units. The De Soto Six chassis also served as the basis for the contemporary Fargo light van.

The Spanish explorer mascot of De Soto.

1930 De Soto CK

Lancia Dilambda
1930, Italy

Lancia had been pioneers of full unitary construction, coil-spring independent front suspension, and the compact, narrow-angle vee engine. All three had featured on their brilliant four-cylinder Lambda, introduced in 1922 and still current eight years later. By contrast, the 4-litre V8 Dilambda was intended to compete in the American luxury market; hence a separate chassis was always used.

It was an extremely robust chassis of 137-inch (3·48 m) wheelbase. Side-members were 15¾-inches (40 cm) deep at the forward end, and there was cruciform bracing; the fuel tank acted as a structural member. A hypoid bevel rear end kept height down. The engine was of overhead-camshaft type, with the blocks at a compact, 24-degree angle. Ignition was by coil, and the pressure lubrication by twin pumps included a supplementary feed for the centralized chassis oiling. The dual-choke carburetter drew fuel from twin electric pumps, and the gearbox

had four forward speeds. Brakes were mechanical; a servo was added early in the Dilambda's career to cope with the two-tonne weight. The car cruised happily at 75 mph (120 km/h).

Though the Depression put paid to hopes of good American sales, the car was popular in Italian official circles, and nearly 1,700 had found buyers by the end of 1932. The model was still quoted as late as 1937.

Peugeot 201

1930, France

France's small cars tended to be bigger than Britain's: distances were longer and roads straighter. This tendency is typified by the 201, an important 1930 newcomer. Over 120,000 were in use by 1935, and another 20,000 would be added to the score before production ceased in 1937.

The 1,122 cc two-bearing side-valve four lived in a chassis of 96½-inch (2·45 m) wheelbase, with five cross-members. The combination of a transverse front spring with quarter-elliptics at the rear was, however, less civilized. Cooling was by thermo-siphon; surprisingly, 12-volt electrics were furnished. Power was transmitted via a three-speed gearbox to a worm-drive back end: modest output and high weight called for a 6·25 : 1 top gear, and the engine was working hard as the maximum of 56 mph (90 km/h) was approached. When the chassis was further extended to take those 7/8-seater *commerciale* bodies beloved of Frenchmen, performance became abysmal.

But the Peugeot could take unlimited abuse, and at 16,800fr in 1931 it undercut all the opposition, including the little Sima-Standard (page 80). Later cars would feature independently-sprung front wheels, and synchromesh gearboxes, as well as some quite attractive fastback coachwork.

The 1930 Peugeot badge.

1930 Peugeot 201

Rolls-Royce's Spirit of Ecstasy mascot, created by Charles Sykes in 1911.

Rolls-Royce Phantom II

1930, Great Britain

In 1930 the 'Best Car in the World' was still unchallenged, though even in that year it ran to only six cylinders as against the 16 of the biggest Cadillac. Nor was the Phantom II the world's most expensive car: £3,000 ($15,000) would buy all but the most exotic versions. Performance was, however, a respectable 80 mph (128 km/h); as much as 90 (145 km/h) was obtainable with lighter coachwork. As for the absence of revolutionary features, this had always been part of Henry Royce's credo. He preferred to take the ideas of others and refine them to his own exacting standards.

On his 1930 big car, for instance, the mechanical servo four-wheel brakes were built under Hispano-Suiza licence, while the latest hypoid bevel rear end was already in use on Packards and Pierce-Arrows on the Atlantic's far shore. The rest was conventional: the 7·7-litre overhead-valve engine featured dual ignition (by magneto and coil). Retained was the Autovac feed of earlier cars, and the radiator shutters were hand-operated; full thermostatic control (along with centralized chassis lubrication, which Royce mistrusted) came later. Rear springing was, however, now semi-elliptic instead of cantilever, while Rolls-Royce would be among the first British makers to adopt the synchromesh gearbox. This was first seen on the smaller 20/25: presumably Phantom IIs would normally be driven by factory-trained chauffeurs who knew how to double-declutch!

Rolls-Royce, of course, made no bodies as yet: the cars depicted in catalogues were merely representative, though the early 1930s were an era of great elegance, admirably exploited by such as coachbuilders as Barker, Hooper and Park Ward. Though by this time the American factory at Springfield was on its last legs (and still making Phantom Is!), a few British-built left-drive Phantom II chassis were made, with central change instead of the traditional right-hand shift.

1930 Rolls-Royce Phantom II

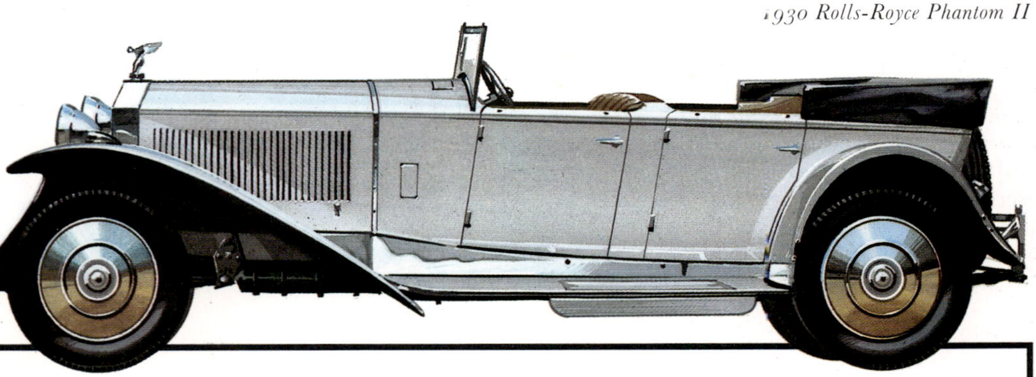

The Phantom II Rolls-Royce chassis, with the latest hypoid rear axle and semi-elliptic rear springing.

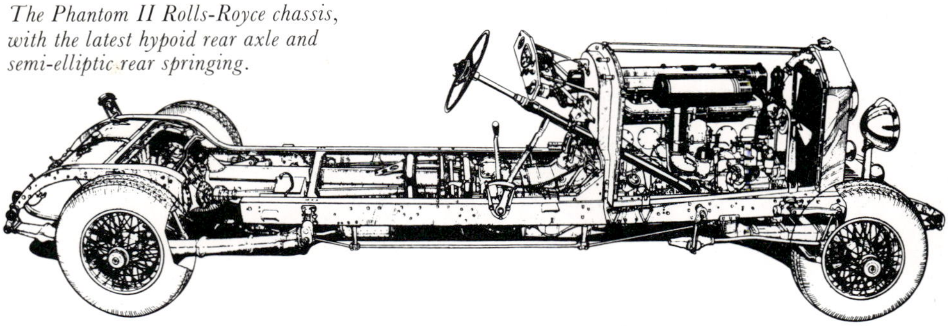

Ruxton

1930, United States

Ruxton's winged radiator cap motif.

Oddly-shaped Wood-Lite headlamps, often fitted by owners of expensive American cars, were standard on Ruxtons.

America bred two front-wheel-drive makes in 1929/30: Cord and Ruxton. The Cord lasted longer, got all the international publicity, and outsold the Ruxton about 10-to-1.

The Ruxton, however, had an engaging history. Named after a financier who decided not to put his shirt on the vehicle after all, it was linked – by motor industry gossip – with eight different manufacturers, all shaky: Gardner, Hupmobile, Jordan, Kissel, Marmon, Moon, Peerless and Stutz. In fact only Kissel and Moon were involved, and both went bankrupt before more than perhaps 500 Ruxtons saw the light of day. Sedan bodies, despite those multi-toned belt mouldings ascribed to interior decorator Joseph Urban, were merely cut-down editions of the Wolseley 21/60 style (by Pressed Steel of Oxford). Swinging instead of winding quarter-lights were necessary because the latter type would have fouled the wheel arches!

Yet the Ruxton was different, for all its three forward speeds, 6-volt electrics, semi-elliptic springs, and internal-expanding hydraulic brakes. True, the engine was Continental's proprietary small straight-eight of 4·3 litres capacity, but it drove the front wheels via an ingenious gearbox on which both weight distribution and length were helped by putting reverse and first in front of the differential, and the two higher ratios behind. The low frame – Ruxton's were said to stand ten inches (25 cm) lower than conventional cars – incorporated no fewer than nine cross-members. Though the dashboard-mounted push-pull gear lever would long be a feature of front-wheel-drive vehicles, on Ruxtons the battery lived under the bonnet, which was of alligator type with fixed sides.

$3,195 (£620) was, however, a lot to pay for an untried design in 1930, and the Ruxton barely saw the year out despite plans to market it in France and England.

Index

Page numbers in *italics* refer to illustrations.